Women Mavericks

Women Mavericks

Celebrating the Success Stories of Indian Women Entrepreneurs

Published by

Gyaanlekha Publishing

Project Curator

Soniyaa Kapoor

Co-Authors

Shanti Sharma, Jyoti Dora, Dr Gagaan, Prakriti Jain, Soundarya Lahari Vedula, Nethra S, Bhagyashri Mhatre, Harshada Singh, Soniyaa Kapoor

Women Mavericks
Shanti Sharma, Jyoti Dora, Dr Gagaan, Prakriti Jain,
Soundarya Lahari Vedula, Nethra S, Bhagyashri Mhatre,
Harshada Singh, Soniyaa Kapoor

Published by
Gyaanlekha Publishing
B 204, Shri Stavan Apartments, Ghodasar,
Ahmedabad, Gujarat – 380050, India

Email: gyaanlekhapublishing@gmail.com

ISBN: 978-81-969715-0-2

Printed in India

First Edition
[October 2024]

Preface

Oh, the strength of a woman!

When I first thought of this project seven years ago, my initial thought was: How about a book that talks about the strength of a woman? I was coming back from a freelance job, listening to music on shuffle, when I came across a beautiful song, "Strength of a Woman." It struck a chord with me. This was when I had just left my well-paying job and a career in a leadership position. I was passionate about doing something meaningful but equally clueless about where I was headed. As I got home and watched the video of this song, I was awestruck. To this day, I'm enchanted by the message and beauty of that song.

What a powerful song, and what a powerful video! Out of habit, I went to the comment section and found it filled with notes from people who had gone through difficult times, sharing how a song, a book, a movie, a friend, or an incident had inspired them to overcome their struggles. It was at that moment that I decided I wanted to curate and publish a book that would speak to the strength of women.

This thought stayed with me all these years, sparking further curiosity. When I started my own entrepreneurial journey and faced tough times, I often found myself reading real-life accounts of people who had found hope during their difficult moments. This strengthened my resolve to curate a book.

As I began promoting this project and talking to women entrepreneurs, I had one clear goal. I didn't want this book to be just a collection of success stories. Who doesn't love a success story? But I wanted to explore the depths of entrepreneurship, particularly in a woman's life. I wanted to highlight the moments of inspiration and the glimmers of hope before starting a business and encourage these entrepreneurs to talk about their failures and challenges.

As I finalise this section of the book, I am so happy to see how it has turned out. The journey of putting this book together has been fascinating. When I first connected with these entrepreneurs over calls, I got to see the richness of their journeys.

Let this book serve as a powerful reminder of your inherent strengths and unwavering resilience, showing how you, too, can overcome challenges and turn your vision into reality. Through the experiences of these extraordinary women, I invite you to rediscover the immense power within you and perhaps find the inspiration to embark on your own entrepreneurial journey.

More than just a collection of stories, this anthology is a treasure trove of inspiration, offering invaluable insights, pivotal learning moments, and a glimpse into the remarkable journeys of persevering entrepreneurs.

Lastly, the journey of curating and producing this book has brought inspiration and positivity to everyone involved. We hand this book over to you with the hope that it will do the same for you, our dear reader!

- Soniyaa Kapoor
Curator, Editor, and Publisher
Gyaanlekha Publishing

Table of Contents

Beyond the Stories
Introducing the Brands of Our Women Mavericks

Women Mavericks

Celebrating the Success Stories
of Indian Women Entrepreneurs!

Who am I?

Shanti Sharma
Founder, Coach, and Facilitator at Grow with Satori

Life is a Camera; face it wearing a smile! This quote by an anonymous person has stuck with me since childhood. Since then, I have faced all my challenges, worries, excitement, and anxiousness with a smile. It has worked for me well, and I hope the smile sails me through as I pour out a part of my life, my entrepreneurial journey, out here for your review. So, with a BIG BIG smile, very warm greetings to all my esteemed readers as we embark together on this literary journey.

The story I am about to share is a part of my journey over the last 50 years, energising and motivating for me as I recount it, with the hope that you'll find some valuable insights for your own entrepreneurial path.

Hi, I'm Shanti Sharma, a coach and leadership facilitator by profession. I'm the proud owner of an organisation called 'Grow with Satori.' The term 'satori' emerged from a family brainstorming session where we sought a name for our business. Among various linguistic explorations, the Japanese term 'satori' resonated deeply with us. In Zen meditation, satori signifies awakening through self-discovery, a concept central to coaching. It's about helping individuals understand who they are, why they behave as they do, and what changes they need to make to align with their chosen path. Thus, Grow with Satori was born.

You might wonder why I'm sharing this narrative. Simply put, developing and growing people is my passion. Whether through my 26+ years of career or my recent years running my own business, I've had the privilege of training, coaching, mentoring, and supporting countless individuals in becoming better versions of themselves. This fills me with immense gratitude and joy, driving me to continue this noble pursuit for decades to come.

The beginning of my Entrepreneurial Journey!

My journey into entrepreneurship began during my time at a multinational corporation. Leading a dedicated team and enjoying a fulfilling role as a learning leader allowed me to grow personally and professionally while nurturing the development of others—a passion close to my heart. As my career progressed, I took pride in the value I brought to the organisation, fuelled by occasional recognition and praise.

In 2018, significant changes shook our organisation. Global leaders convened in India operations/headquarters to discuss a major transformation. As the learning team representative, I engaged in intense discussions and presentations, envisioning growth opportunities for our India team, including potential promotions for many, including myself.

The months that followed were filled with eager anticipation as we awaited confirmation of the proposed changes. However, December came and went without any updates, leaving us to speculate about the delay. As January dawned, optimism still prevailed, with hopes pinned on the imminent announcement of positive news.

Yet, January 29, 2019, marked a watershed moment—one that would forever alter the trajectory of my professional journey. Stepping into the office that day, I was met with a sombre atmosphere as whispers of restructuring permeated the air. Concerned glances and hushed conversations hinted at the gravity of the situation, setting the stage for what would unfold next.

As I made my way to my workstation, I encountered a scene of palpable distress. Some wore expressions of disbelief and confusion, and two of my team members were in tears. With twenty meters separating me from my workstation, each step felt like a journey in itself.

Arriving at my workstation, I wasted no time delving into the heart of the matter. Opening my laptop, I navigated to the email containing the new organisational structure, hoping for a semblance of normalcy amidst the chaos. However, what greeted me on the screen defied belief—a glaring absence of the India team, relegating us to the periphery of the organisation's plans.

Stunned and reeling from the revelation, I reached out to my manager for clarification, only to be met with uncertainty and confusion on his end as well. With no answers forthcoming, I found myself grappling with the enormity of the situation, tasked with providing reassurance and guidance to my team members in the face of overwhelming uncertainty.

As the reality of our predicament sank in, I resolved to take action in the ensuing days. Mobilising my team, I initiated efforts to update resumes and explore internal opportunities within the organisation. Simultaneously, I embarked on a mission to advocate for our value and contributions to the India management team, underscoring our critical role in the organisation's success. Despite the challenges that lay ahead, I remained steadfast in my commitment to supporting my team members in their quest for new opportunities, whether within or outside the organisation.

Recognising that without us, the learning team, they might not be able to deliver any training customised to India, the Indian Management Team decided to retain a part of my team. A very small part, albeit four of us, including myself, remained part of the India learning team. However, the experience served as a catalyst for introspection, prompting me to question the fragility of traditional employment and the inherent risks associated with placing one's fate in the hands of external forces.

Thus, the seeds of entrepreneurship were planted—a nascent desire for autonomy and self-determination taking root within me. Though unprepared for the arduous journey that lay ahead, the resolve to carve out my own path and reclaim control over my professional destiny became my beacon of hope, guiding me toward a future defined by purpose and possibility.

How I prepared myself for Entrepreneurship

Just having a dream isn't enough; it is important to have a plan to make your dream come true. So, what was my plan? First, I had to ensure that my financial pressures were controllable. To achieve this, I took significant steps such as selling some properties, putting the money in the bank, reducing EMIs by transferring them to banks offering better interest rates, and so on. The goal was to minimise EMIs and maintain financial stability.

Secondly, financial preparation was crucial for embarking on my entrepreneurial journey. So, I began saving large amounts of money with the intent of feeling financially secure enough to maintain our lifestyle even if I didn't earn for a year and a half into my entrepreneurial journey.

However, what about my entrepreneurial journey itself? That thought kept looming until one day I recalled my experience delivering a coaching course for managers in a previous organisation. I remembered how much I enjoyed discussing coaching principles, ethics, and the art of questioning. Inspired by this realisation, I began inquiring and learning from coaches around me, only to realise that I needed to start my coaching journey from scratch with training, practice, mentoring, and supervision. So be it! I enrolled in my first coach training course.

By the end of 2020, I became a certified coach, which boosted my confidence and reaffirmed that I was on the right path. But I wasn't ready to settle; I continued learning, training, and practising to gain additional certifications and enhance my coaching skills.

The third aspect of preparation involved readying my family for the upcoming changes. This meant explaining the uncertainties of income and involving them in financial planning discussions to ensure everyone understood and supported the journey ahead. It was reassuring to receive unwavering support from my immediate family, although I faced significant pushback from my extended family. In fact, my father was doubtful about sustenance without a regular salary in the bank. He offered to help financially too. Others in the family who had never ventured into entrepreneurship tried to talk me out, suggesting that I retain a safe and well-paying job. It took lots of effort, discussions, arguments, and confrontation before a few gave up, and a few understood my perspective.

The last thing to manage before I submitted my resignation to my current organisation was to ensure that my team was well-equipped to function and perform in my absence. My preparation had started, and my team members knew of my plans and wholeheartedly supported me in my journey. They levelled up and stepped up to perform, learn, grow, and challenge themselves until eventually, I found myself to be redundant. I realised I did not have to do anything, and the time was right for me to submit my resignation.

Seeking guidance from seasoned entrepreneurs, who became my mentors, was invaluable. Their advice ranged from building my brand and visibility on social media to acquiring low-paid clients and strategically timing my resignation to minimise tax liability. In 2022, with the support and encouragement of my family and mentors, I took the leap, submitting my resignation to pursue my passion for coaching and training wholeheartedly.

The Journey Itself

On May 27th, 2022, I bid farewell to my corporate job, surrounded by flowers, gifts, and the warmth of friends accompanying me home. However, amidst the joyous occasion, a call from my brother jolted me back to reality – he urgently needed my insurance number as our father was in the hospital. Feeling helpless, I regretted having submitted my resignation. I reminded my brother that I did not have a job and thereby no insurance. Despite this setback, my brother remained unfazed, suggesting alternatives and assuring me that all would be fine. It indeed was fine.

This incident underscored the importance of corporate benefits, such as monthly financial security and medical insurance, which I would no longer enjoy. Consequently, my husband and I prioritised securing proper medical insurance despite the hefty premiums. This is one tip I'd give to everybody, whether corporate employees, homemakers, or entrepreneurs: Have your own medical insurance; don't just depend on corporate-provided insurance.

I insisted on having a dedicated workspace to maintain the discipline and rhythm of office life. I received lots of discouragement from acquaintances and friends who reminded me that I was planning to spend even before earning. However, I was clear, I did not want to let go of the rhythm and rigour of going to the office. It would be my sacred place where worries and stresses of home relations and friends are left outside the door, and I'm able to focus on just the thing I like to do. This has indeed paid off. Team members who eventually joined me in my entrepreneurial journey were more comfortable seeing that there was a workplace. I was able to show off my workspace to my clients as they came over for meetings. I could claim this space as my own.

As I delved into entrepreneurship, I found myself inundated with administrative tasks, detracting from my passion for coaching and training. Recognising this, I assembled a team comprising former colleagues, friends, and neighbours, delegating tasks beyond my expertise.

Embracing collaboration, I cultivated a network of coaches and trainers, expanding my reach and service offerings. Moreover, I learned to gracefully accept help, whether from my husband in managing finances or from peers offering collaboration opportunities. Yet another tip I'd offer to all entrepreneurs is not to overwhelm themselves with doing everything all by themselves. Rather, gather a team of experts who can support you while you focus on your core and your passion. This also means gracefully accepting help when offered and not trying to be that superwoman who dies at the end of a marvellous heroic adventure.

I also learnt that collaborations are key for entrepreneurs. Through collaboration, I not only expanded my business but also fostered mutually beneficial relationships with other coaches and facilitators. I now have a bunch of coaches and facilitators who enable me to offer scaled-up services to my clients. They also are a strong support system when I need them most. These collaborations and partnerships have also opened doors for newer businesses trickling in.

As an entrepreneur, I've learned that being a leader in a corporate setting is much easier than leading in an enterprise. It requires a delicate balance of being both people-centric and business-centric. If you focus too much on the business, your team becomes demotivated, and if your team is demotivated, your business naturally starts to crumble. While I have yet to discover the secret sauce, I remain open to seeking feedback whenever I struggle to maintain this balance. I ask my team for input, show my vulnerable self, and am grateful for their guidance, support, and willingness to help.

Another realisation is that the past few years have been a journey of independence, not just for me but for my children as well. I've worked hard to teach them independence in all aspects of life, knowing that my schedule would soon become busier, leaving me with fewer hours to spare for them. Fortunately, both my kids are now fully independent, capable of taking care of themselves, and even supporting me when needed. Of course, this preparation started right at the beginning when I shared the thought of starting my business with my family and kids.

Finally, another tip for fellow entrepreneurs: continue to prioritise your growth and development. Not only do I ensure that I complete at least one certification or take up a course to enhance my skills as a trainer or coach every year, but I also encourage my team to do the same. I incentivise them for their contributions to the business, whether it's bringing in new clients, generating leads, delivering projects, or building strong customer relationships. By focusing on creating and nurturing a great team, we strengthen our business and foster a culture of continuous learning and growth.

Way Forward

This is just the beginning. It's a long journey ahead and an arduous one indeed. With all the help, support, vulnerability, determination, and resilience, I hope to traverse this journey. My dream is to set up a large training coaching consultancy firm that can cater to the needs of several audiences - be it youngsters seeking guidance on their career choices, people struggling to maintain relationships at home or work, leaders grappling with team growth and grooming, or business leaders struggling with the strategy to grow their businesses. I know I can do this with the support of my network - the mentors, cheerleaders, champions, and guides that I have gathered for myself to support me through this journey.

I don't hope to traverse this journey alone, but I do intend to pave the way for myself.
- Shanti Sharma

~~~
~~~

AUTHOR INTRODUCTION

Shanti Sharma is the Founder, Coach, and Facilitator at Grow with Satori. Developing people is her passion, and she considers herself fortunate to live her passion every day by enabling people to realise their true potential and supporting them in translating their potential into meaningful work and relationships that support building high-performing teams and organisations.

Shanti is an ICF Certified (PCC) Coach, EMCC accredited Sr. Practitioner, Certified Mentor Coach (MCCP), Certified Learning and Development Manager (CLDM), NLP practitioner, Transactional Analysis (TA) Practitioner, and a seasoned Learning professional with over 27 years of experience. Out of her total experience, 24+ years have been dedicated to Learning and Development (L&D). Her experience ranges from end-to-end management of the L&D function to supporting organisational development initiatives. With a breadth of experience across various industries such as IT, BPO, and Banking, and having managed small to very large multi-location complex projects.

Shanti is a Tamilian born in Nagpur and brought up in Delhi, is married to a Rajasthani Sharma family and has been settled in Bangalore for the past 16 years. She has two lovely children: an elder daughter who is an illustrator and a younger son who is majoring in Psychology.

Connect with Shanti Sharma, Grow with Satori:

Webpage: www.growithsatori.com
Email: shanti@growithsatori.com
LinkedIn: www.linkedin.com/in/shantisharma
Linktree: www.linktr.ee/growtihsatori
Instagram: @growithsatori
Twitter: LearningSatori
Facebook: growithsatori

***

The Courage to Create

Jyoti Dora
Founder, Readers Adda

Kaani Kaani Kantoni, Bainth podlo Anthony...if only I could explain the emotions that this line from a popular Konkani story stirs in my heart every time it crosses my mind. The number of times I had requested my granny to tell me this story, and each time, she narrated it with a chuckle. The story comprised a series of questions, each leading to the next part.

Have you seen a child with her father at the bookstore on a railway station? That would be me. Every vacation and travel would mean travelling by train, thereby the railway station and the bookstore visit. Books ranging from Tinkle to Akbar Birbal and Tenali Rama. Never did my dad refuse to buy me books from the Book Depot.

Back home, I always saw my dad reading newspapers and Mom with her Kannada magazines. Since I was raised in Surat, Gujarat, I can speak my mother tongue, Konkani, but can't read or speak Kannada. So, whenever I saw Mom reading, I would nudge her to read out the cartoon strips to me, which she would read and translate into Konkani for me. Not only that, she would also read out other meaningful stories to me, thereby laying a strong foundation for character building.

Bengalis are said to have a great love for literature, and I learned this from my experience with my uncle. He used to subscribe to a lot of magazines and buy amazing books for both his daughters, who were just a few years younger than me. When vacation came, I would hop over to their house first and bask in the company of the books they had collected throughout the year. I breathed books.

At school, we had a library period as well as a dance period. Students were allowed to choose between these two. For dance, a separate fee had to be paid. I paid for the dance period and happily settled myself at the library.

The only time I was asked to leave my Economics class in college was because I was reading Shakespeare. I had been reading the book in the library, and when it was time for Economics class, I went to the class but could not resist the temptation to continue reading.

Working with corporate companies led me to buy and read management books. While conducting programs for expecting mothers and kids, I started reading self-help books, and while teaching at a school, I explored Fiction all over again.

And today, I'm surrounded by over 20,000 books. So, to connect the dots, we seldom look at life as a movie in the making. It's only when something substantial happens that we are able to see where it all came from.

I started my career in corporate companies as most youngsters aspire and consider that to be the path to growth and development. Right from Office Automation to FMCG to Telecom and ISP, to MLM to retailing, to educator to entrepreneur. I am blessed to have witnessed and lived this journey firsthand. Initially, the idea of career growth was so strong that I chose to move away from family for better job prospects. I lived away from my husband even after a love marriage so that I wouldn't miss the race. Just to realise that home is where the heart is. At one point, I came to the conclusion that I would like to be a homemaker and take care of our house, and thus quit my high-paying banking job to join my husband at a remote location. To be honest, I loved the place. The homemaker journey did not last over a month, so I joined an MLM company and, within three months, qualified for a Kathmandu contest. Life had different plans for us; his job led him to various cities, and I readily moved with him, seeking something that would keep me engaged and that I would enjoy doing. That's how I opened up Brain Development centres, and eventually, when I had a daughter, I donned the hat of a hands-on Mom.

With a new life on hand began the journey of a mompreneur. From day one, my husband Rohit and I were very clear that we would plan and do anything and everything around our daughter. Hence, I started selling sarees and kurtis from home, fitting it into the time available after tending to my little one's needs. We had ample time for playing, craft activities, and reading aloud. At one point, Charvi was surrounded by over 600 books. Whenever I visited a book fair with her, I just couldn't leave without picking at least 90-100 books, without batting an eye at the payment counter. What was picked was mine, and I wouldn't want to leave a few to reduce the bill. Which I do when I'm buying clothes.

Now, the key was to spread books throughout the house within Charvi's reach. There were books in her playroom, in the bedrooms, on the side table, on the centre table, and in all other possible places, which led her to pick up books more than anything else.

As soon as she began schooling, I joined a school too. Again, taking language and literature classes, I realised the struggle children were facing despite studying in English medium schools. While their vocabularies were not developed, they even lacked ideas to build upon a context. The children who were into the habit of reading were able to write much better than their peers. The moment I settled in this new role, destiny called us to Ahmedabad, and I resisted. I wanted the feeling of satisfaction and stability in work and shared this with my husband. For another year, Charvi and I stayed back in Rajkot.

Children are not roadblocks—they empower us. They push us to become better…do more…love more.

As luck would have it, within a month of shifting to Ahmedabad, we moved to Surat. This was when people started noticing Charvi with books at most times, and they started asking me how I had managed to raise a reader while their children were hooked to gadgets. That did it! The idea of helping other children explore the beautiful and enriching habit of reading mulled in my mind.

I had sleepless nights thinking about how I could create a program to help empower children and impact their choices. Within two months, we came up with a program and shared it with the women's group of my society. There was no response for a week. One day while returning from a friend's place, I saw a group of women sitting and chatting. The moment they saw me, one of them called me and asked what the message was about. I explained and got two confirmations for registration on the spot.

Over the next month, we had ten kids coming over. I realised that, although I had specified the program was for kids aged 4-14, most of the children were around 4-5 years old. They couldn't read by themselves, so I started reading stories to them. They enjoyed it, but I felt something was missing. This wasn't what I wanted. I reworked the program, and the revised version became a big hit. Today, even after nearly seven years, kids who join us at four can confidently navigate through the pages of books by themselves. We trained them to read and helped them with pronunciation, word meanings, and comprehension.

Within three months, we were up with two reading centres and 81 kids through word of mouth.

In the second year, we had four centres running successfully, and then the COVID-19 Pandemic struck. During the lockdown, I resisted using the online platform initially, but encouragement from associates and parents helped me adapt to the situation, and we began conducting the classes online. I experienced the power of the digital medium for the first time when children joined us from Africa, Ahmedabad, Bangalore, Gandhinagar, Gandhidham, Delhi, Mumbai, Orissa, and different parts of Surat, which I could otherwise not cater to. During this time too, I found myself constantly buying books from various online sources like Amazon, Flipkart, and various sales groups. I was asked why I was investing so much in books since we already had a collection of nearly 4000 books by then. The question hit me hard, and I launched doorstep library services after learning that children were not allowed in local libraries during this period. Also, I realised that even though children are enrolled in library services, parents seldom find time to take children to the library. Even when they did, they hadn't the faintest idea of which books to pick or what level of reading their child was at. Today we have a collection of over 20,000 books, and the collection hosts books for all age groups, right from infants to adults.

It was the same time when I was planning a World record with kids from various schools participating in a reading activity, and when we approached a few schools, we could see the worry they had in even asking for a minimal sum from parents for the certification. During one of our conversations, I mentioned that my daughter Charvi is an avid reader and has read lot many books. Something struck. I took Charvi with me to the centre every day and set aside books that she said she had read and remembered. My decision to set aside those books was backed by her confidence. We could set aside as many as 2020 books as all the books she had read before the setting up of Readers Adda were passed on to colleagues and cousins. The books she selected ranged from Harry Potter and Percy Jackson to books written by Sudha Murty to Ruskin Bond. She also asked me to keep some of Tinkle Digests and Amar Chitra Katha aside. The process required us to share the list of books and present them in front of the adjudicator allotted by the World Talent Organization. In the presence of witnesses, Charvi was asked to summarise nearly 41 books randomly picked by the adjudicator from the 2000+ books presented. She was allowed five lapses, and to our great delight, she did not take a single lapse. The record for being the youngest to read the maximum number of books was established at the age of ten. Her felicitation by the World Talent Organization was a year later, and it was a memorable one as we, the mother-daughter duo, were felicitated on the same stage. While hers was known, mine came as a surprise. We actively promoted the importance of reading through various seminars at different school groups as well as community groups during the lockdown period. This selfless activity did not go unnoticed, and I was awarded by the World Talent Organization as the Most Inspiring Human for my services rendered in spreading awareness of the benefits of reading. The icing on the cake was donating over 1000 books to mark this occasion to nearby Anganwadi and help centres we knew. What made it special was that during lockdown Charvi and I were enrolled for a lot of online courses and created a program which was led by Charvi. The fees collected from the batch were then utilised to purchase these books.

She was later felicitated on many different platforms, and one such platform was JCI 40 under 40. This further strengthened our conviction on the power of this most enriching habit.

Post Pandemic, we resumed with two centres as we decided we wanted more time on hand to cater to Charvi's growing requirement of our time and presence.

Year 2024, and we are well into the 7th year of operations and going strong. We also organise book fairs at schools now. We have been successful in establishing ourselves as a sought-after name for reading activities and witness amazing results regularly. We have impacted over 10000 lives through seminars, reading programs, and book fairs. Every effort is being made to reach families more effectively and make reading resources available to kids by educating parents.

Some interesting observations made during book fairs were that parents were keen on activity books and books that supported academic studies, while children were more inclined towards story books, novels, and books that gave them knowledge about the world around them. It takes efforts to educate parents on the importance of reading out to their young children much before the children can read for themselves. To surround them with books so that they start associating books with fun and not merely as an academic requirement. Let their imaginations soar with the characters of the stories and visit distant lands. All this while making the children more confident, enhancing their imagination and creativity as well as focus and concentration. Also, in households where English is hardly spoken, reading helps children acquire rich vocabulary and ideas without much effort. A child who reads regularly also speaks and writes better.

Over the years, our story has been covered by various media, and we have been awarded as the most eminent business entrepreneur as well as 15 top women entrepreneurs to reckon with. At this juncture, my heart is filled with gratitude for all those who believed in me and the concept, especially parents of kids who are associated with Readers Adda through Reading Programs, Doorstep Library service, and Book Fairs. Parents who ensured that their children came regularly for the reading sessions throughout the year and constantly renewed their membership with us, as well as spread the word for our services, helped us grow year after year and proved to be the backbone for us to move ahead strong and robust.

In our attempt to impact many more lives and be easily accessible to parents who understand the impact of reading on the current and upcoming generations more than ever, we are now ready with our Franchise Deck and looking forward to empowering women who believe in the magic of reading and join in a profession that's not only lucrative but also has a strong social impact. At this juncture, my husband Rohit and I are Directors of JRD EDUHUB PRIVATE LIMITED and working towards taking Readers Adda throughout India, beginning with more locations at Surat in the first phase.

The courage to press the reset button at every phase and stage of life, under any condition, was only possible because I had found a strong pillar of faith in Rohit. Living in a relationship of equals, right from shouldering the responsibilities at home, parenting Charvi, or finances, there was never the slightest bit of doubt in his eyes or expressions for anything that I ever wanted to do. Most times, only the words 'Kar Lo' were more than enough to get me going.

Inspired by our Prime Minister Narendra Modi Ji's talk on Mann ki Baat, where he urged storytellers to narrate stories of freedom fighters to our young children, I wish to bring it to fruition through a book that I'm penning with brief stories highlighting the lives and specific traits that these young minds could adapt as guiding light to brighten their own path and the nation at large.

"There are many little ways to enlarge your child's world. Love of books is the best of all." - Jacqueline Kennedy.
"There's no such thing as a kid who hates reading. There are kids who love reading, and kids who are reading the wrong books." - James Patterson.
- Jyoti Dora

~~~
~~~

AUTHOR INTRODUCTION

Ms. Jyoti Dora, the founder of Readers Adda, is a Certified Storyteller, NLP Practitioner, and Transformation Coach with an MHRD degree. Her career includes roles in major corporations like Idea, PepsiCo, British Broadband, and ABN AMRO BANK, focusing on Customer Empathy and Sales. She also served as an educator at Galaxy International School, renowned for its innovative educational methods.

Jyoti's journey into reading advocacy began with her research on children's perceptions of books and her personal experience with her daughter Charvi. Observing Charvi's transformation into an avid reader, Jyoti confirmed that regular reading enhances language skills, communication, confidence, and academic performance while reducing screen time. This led her to create a comprehensive Reading Program for children aged 4-14.

Since moving to Surat in 2017, Jyoti has committed herself to combating gadget addiction and fostering a love of reading. Readers Adda provides an engaging learning environment, supporting both dependent and independent readers. With over 20 years of diverse experience, Jyoti is dedicated to impacting children across Surat and India, helping them develop into confident leaders through the joy of reading.

Connect with Jyoti Dora, Readers Adda:

Webpage: www.readersadda.co.in
Email: jyotidora21@gmail.com
LinkedIn: www.linkedin.com/in/jyoti-dora-67230719b
Facebook: www.facebook.com/jyoti.dora.12
www.facebook.com/readersaddasurat
Instagram: jyotidora.readersadda

***

The Journey of an Unlikely Entrepreneur

Dr Gagaan
Founder Uniqaya lifestyle |
Director Unimarck Pharma I Ltd

Most entrepreneurs you come across seem to have a burning desire to achieve a specific goal, something that drives them relentlessly. But for me, it was different. I always wanted to be a homemaker. Growing up in a very happy home, I was never career-conscious, nor did I have any dreams of becoming a "lady boss." My focus was always on family and maintaining the warmth and joy of the household.

You might have heard the famous quote: "When you want something with all your heart, the entire universe conspires to help you achieve it." For me, it worked in the opposite direction. I ended up pursuing a path I had never imagined for myself. In the beginning, I thought this was some kind of twist of fate, but over time, I realised that it was a necessary step toward self-discovery and growth.

Before I delve further into my journey, allow me to introduce myself: I am Dr Gagaan, a mother turned doctor, turned healer, and now an entrepreneur. Believe me when I say the journey has not been as simple as it might sound in this brief introduction. There were struggles, challenges, and moments of doubt. But through it all, I found my way and discovered my purpose.

A Search for Self-Love

From a young age, I faced comments about my appearance. Unlike the rest of my family, who had very fair complexions, my skin was darker. I still remember the looks and whispers. Though my family loved and supported me, society was not always as kind. I was often given nicknames like "Kalo," which means "dark-skinned." At that age, I did not realise it, but these comments stayed with me, and over time, they became a catalyst for my fascination with skincare.

I began exploring skincare recipes, reading about natural ingredients, and researching what could help me feel more confident and presentable. Growing up during the era when Shahnaz Husain was revered as the queen of herbal skincare, I devoured beauty magazines looking for tips and tricks. Back then, Google was not an option, so I relied on printed media and word of mouth. Slowly, I developed a deep knowledge of Indian herbs and their benefits.

Even as life took different turns, my interest in skincare and natural remedies remained. I earned a degree in science, but before I could think of pursuing anything further, I got married. Unfortunately, the marriage did not last, and soon, I found myself navigating life as a single mother. While raising my child, I decided to continue my education and earned my doctorate in naturopathy. This new phase of my life opened doors to spiritual growth and healing modalities like past life regression, tarot readings, and crystal healing. I began helping others heal, but eventually, I felt a calling to stop. The universe seemed to be nudging me toward something else.

A New Path Emerges

In January 2019, while visiting my son in Canada, I had a conversation that changed my life. He said, “Mom, you have dedicated your life to me. I think it is time for you to start pursuing your own dreams.” His words struck a chord with me. On my flight back to India, I could not stop thinking about what my dreams really were. What had I always wanted but never pursued?

Shortly after returning home, I serendipitously connected with someone who specialised in helping people build online businesses. During our conversations, we talked about skincare, and it was then that I realised I had a treasure trove of knowledge and passion inside me. I had spent years experimenting with natural ingredients and formulations myself, and now, it was time to turn that passion into something tangible. My family was fully supportive—especially since we had been in the pharmaceutical business for 40 years. They encouraged me to take the leap and start a new vertical within the business. That is how UNIQAYA was born.

The Birth of UNIQAYA

The name UNIQAYA was not chosen at random. It reflects my deep-rooted belief in authenticity and quality. I wanted my brand to represent something more than just skincare. The prefix "Uni" symbolises uniqueness, emphasising that each person is special in their own way and deserves skincare that enhances their beauty, both inside and out. "Kaya," which means body or skin in Sanskrit, was added to reflect the holistic approach to wellness that had been a constant in my life. UNIQAYA, then, is not just about skincare; it is about embracing and celebrating the uniqueness of each individual.

When it came to the look and feel of the products, I wanted to create something that was premium yet approachable. I have been exposed to international products all my life and have always admired their quality and aesthetic. I chose a deep blue colour scheme to evoke a sense of luxury while keeping the products affordable and functional. For me, it was important that UNIQAYA deliver international-level quality without alienating anyone in terms of price.

The COVID-19 Challenge

Just as our vision was taking shape, the COVID-19 pandemic hit. It was a time of unprecedented uncertainty and upheaval.

Businesses around the world were shutting down, supply chains were disrupted, and life as we knew it was turned upside down. The vendors we were working with suddenly doubled and tripled their prices, and the lockdown made it nearly impossible to proceed with our launch as intended.

At that moment, promoting a skincare line felt inappropriate. The world was focused on survival, and talking about skincare seemed trivial in comparison. However, amidst the chaos, the surge in online activity presented an unexpected opportunity. As people adapted to the "new normal," they turned to digital platforms for shopping, work, and social interaction.

Though I was initially reluctant to advertise our products, I began to notice something interesting: prolonged screen time was taking a toll on people's skin. With virtual meetings, online classes, and remote work becoming the norm, individuals were spending more time in front of screens than ever before. This increased exposure to blue light led to various skin issues, including dullness, dryness, and sensitivity.

An Innovative Solution

This realisation sparked an innovative idea. I recognised the need for a product that addressed these new skincare concerns, specifically protecting against both the harmful effects of the sun and the blue light emitted by digital devices. Drawing on my background in naturopathy and my commitment to creating functional, effective solutions, I developed a unique sunscreen that not only provided UV protection but also shielded the skin from the damaging effects of blue light.

Creating this sunscreen was no easy task. The formulation had to be light, non-greasy, and suitable for all skin types. We sourced the best ingredients known for their protective and nourishing properties, ensuring the final product met the highest standards. This sunscreen, which protects against both sun and screen, became one of our bestselling products.

The launch of this product, during a time when the world was grappling with a global crisis, was both a challenge and a triumph. The positive feedback we received from customers validated the importance of adapting to changing needs and reaffirmed our commitment to creating products that genuinely improve the lives of those who use them.

A Testament to Resilience

The journey of UNIQAYA has been one of constant learning and adaptation. The pandemic forced us to think differently, innovate, and respond to the evolving needs of our customers. It also taught us the importance of resilience. As an entrepreneur, every day presents new challenges, but it is the love and trust of our customers that keeps me going.

UNIQAYA is not just a skincare brand. It is a testament to the belief that beauty comes from embracing your uniqueness. Through our products, we aim to empower people to feel confident in their own skin and to recognise the power of self-love. We blend natural ingredients with cutting-edge formulations to create products that are not only effective but also nurturing.

As I continue to navigate this journey, I remain committed to delivering the best for our customers. The experience has taught me that the entrepreneurial path is not just about building a business—it is about creating something that makes a difference in people's lives. Through UNIQAYA, I hope to inspire others to embrace their uniqueness and let their inner glow shine.

- Dr Gagaan

AUTHOR INTRODUCTION

Dr Gagaan, the founder of Uniqaya Lifestyle, is a dynamic professional with a rich and diverse background. After completing her B.Sc., she pursued a career in exterior and interior design, where she had the privilege of working with renowned architects. However, her passion for holistic healing led her to pursue post-graduation in Naturopathy from Punjab University. This marked a turning point in her career, as she joined her family's business, Unimarck Pharmaceuticals (the parent company of Uniqaya), where she took on key roles in pre-medical training and product development.

In addition to her professional achievements, Dr Gagaan is also deeply connected to spirituality. She is a certified Past Life Regression (PLR) therapist, trained in the lineage of Brian Weiss and Dr Newton, as well as a Magnified Healer and Melchizedek Healer. Her skills as a card reader further complement her healing practices.

Outside of her professional and spiritual life, Dr Gagaan enjoys cooking, gardening, and creating Tanjore paintings. She also loves long drives with good music. Her compassion extends to her support for NGOs like DIR India, where she contributes to the nutritional needs of young orphans, showcasing her commitment to giving back to society.

Connect with Dr Gagaan, Uniqaya:

Instagram: @uniqayalifestyle @gaganbhaatia26
Facebook: www.facebook.com/Uniqayalifestyle
LinkedIn: www.linkedin.com/in/drgaganbhatia
www.linkedin.com/company/uniqayalifestyle
Website: www.uniqaya.com
Linktree: https://www.linktr.ee/drgaganbhatia

Sarees, Struggles and Success: The Making of Piharwa

Prakriti Jain
Founder and Brand Owner, Piharwa

As I reflect on my journey as an entrepreneur, I feel grateful, humbled, and a little nervous. While many people start their businesses with clear plans and goals, my path was different. It wasn't something I planned—it was more a combination of love and career. I left a stable corporate job and, almost by default, joined my husband Aakash's finance business.

Aakash started AB Leasing and Finance Ltd, where his strong business sense and vision for growth were evident. With his guidance, I began to learn the ropes of running a business and took my first steps as an entrepreneur.

This journey was not only about work or business but also about my personal growth and transformation. My earlier experiences in Pune and work travel exposed me to different corporate cultures. Yet, nothing prepared me for the challenges of entrepreneurship in Bhopal and Jabalpur.

Navigating the difficulties of arranged marriage while also trying to establish myself as a working woman came with its own set of challenges. As I adjusted to this change and adapted to my new life, I found it challenging to adapt to Aakash's work style and approach, as the finance business felt very technical and lacked the creative elements I enjoyed. While we worked well together and maintained a strong partnership, there were moments of friction. It was hard for me to fully express my creativity and use my skills in such a structured and methodical environment, which made it difficult to reach my full potential.

This push and pull persisted for five years and beyond. As I had moments of frustration and self-doubt, a realisation began to dawn on me. I was only following instructions without embracing the true essence of entrepreneurship. Once I acknowledged these thoughts, my journey of self-discovery and forging my own path amidst the shadows of our primary company began.

Amidst my responsibilities at our current company, I felt a strong desire for creative expression. During 2009-2010, I started to think about a new venture and the possibility of letting my creativity flourish. Unexpectedly, an opportunity arose during the joyful and chaotic time of my brother Vikas's wedding. While preparing for the wedding, I visited many saree shops in Bhopal. I felt dissatisfied, which sparked a realisation about the gap between market offerings and customer demand.

I had not forgotten about this even after returning from the wedding, and a sudden call from Vikas asking me to join him in Mumbai for a franchise fair set the wheels in motion. With anticipation, I perused the pages of the Times of India and mapped out my journey to Nehru Centre at Worli.

As I stepped into the busy venue, a variety of business opportunities greeted me, nudging me closer to my dream of entrepreneurship. One franchise stood out: a well-known clothing brand with roots stretching back a century. I spoke with their representatives, eager to learn more about their time-honoured brand and excited about the possibilities for my own business.

I returned filled with excitement and determination but met with some scepticism from my family. Our family was naturally concerned about this new direction, as none of us were accustomed to the retail side of the business, having always worked in a white-collar space. The idea of stepping into retail entrepreneurship was unfamiliar, and they had understandable concerns about meeting new people, the long and demanding work hours, and forming partnerships with those outside our usual circle.

I understood where their fear was coming from. I decided to clear my family's doubts and prepared a detailed project report supported by projections and strategies. I shared my vision with them and highlighted the untapped market potential and how it could strengthen our collective growth and wealth. I persisted in my efforts despite their response to my excitement.

On April 8th, 2011, filled with excitement and nerves, I began my entrepreneurial journey by signing the contract. This accomplishment filled me with hope and boundless possibilities, leaving me blissfully unaware of the weight of responsibility that lay ahead.

The initial years were thrilling and filled with challenges as well as successes. I worked enthusiastically to promote the brand and establish a name for ourselves in the market. Despite my tireless efforts, I found meeting my clients' ever-changing and unique demands challenging.

As the initial joy and excitement of entrepreneurship began to fade, I faced the harsh reality of shifting market dynamics. In just two to three years, I observed a significant shift in customer preferences. I realised that the offerings provided by the franchise model no longer aligned with the refined tastes of my clientele.

Each day, the gap between customers' expectations and available inventory widened. What was once a thriving business started to make me feel discontent. Despite my sincere efforts to close this gap, the hierarchy of the franchise system turned out to be a major obstacle. While there were temporary solutions, the main problem remained unsolved.

Despite my sincere efforts, the gap between me and the principal franchise increased day by day. As a result, our sales figures dropped, reflecting the dissatisfaction of our clients. We were no longer considered a beacon of style and sophistication; instead, the store earned a reputation for being overpriced and out of touch with the market's evolving tastes.

Faced with these challenges, I decided to take matters into my own hands. If the franchise model could not deliver the quality and variety my customers demanded, I would source it myself. This marked my transition from a franchisee to an independent entrepreneur.

I immersed myself in the intricate world of sarees, exploring everything from colour combinations and designs to fabric and weaving techniques. While I did not have a formal education in fashion or weaving, I learned through the challenges and shifts of marketplaces and the demands of various clients. My hometown, Jaipur, became the hub for finding and sourcing unique, high-quality products. Amidst the bustling streets of Jaipur's market, I discovered treasures that would soon adorn the racks of my growing business. Each transaction and interaction with artisans and vendors taught me valuable lessons in entrepreneurship.

As the curated collection resonated with my clients and received a positive response, a seed of possibility took root within me and ignited a new fire. Why merely source what my customers wanted when I could create it myself? The seeds of my own brand were sown, fuelled by a singular vision: to offer my customers the exquisite craftsmanship and timeless elegance they craved.

While managing the chaos of a few personal relationships and friendships changing and breaking apart, I started the challenging work of establishing my own brand. The franchisee's signboard was dismantled and replaced by the emblem of Piharwa – a beacon of tradition, craftsmanship, and conscious living.

On January 13th, 2017, the seeds of Piharwa were sown, marking the beginning of a new era in handloom sarees and fabrics. With each passing day, our brand gained appreciation and recognition from customers who valued the essence of timeless elegance woven into every thread. As Piharwa flourished, I continued to dream bigger. I envisioned expanding into new areas, leading to the birth of ELEMENTS OF PIHARWA in October 2019, which focused on a broader, holistic lifestyle experience. This launch marked a significant milestone in our journey, opening up new possibilities for growth and expansion. With an unwavering focus on quality and craftsmanship, we curated a collection of handcrafted lifestyle products that spoke to the soul of our brand, resonating with clients who shared our pursuit of mindful living.

Launching Piharwa made me proud, but being a woman in a male-dominated industry came with challenges. Despite building the foundation of a brand that stood for tradition, craftsmanship, and beauty, there were times when I felt like I had to work twice as hard just to be taken seriously. I remember, especially in the early days, walking into meetings with weavers or suppliers and seeing the scepticism in their eyes. I often faced questions like: "Who else has come with you?" or "Are you sure you can place the order and understand the designs?" It was frustrating and intimidating to be second-guessed because of my gender, as if my commitment and ability to run a business were somehow in doubt.

We often say that times have changed, but how much have they really changed? Even though businesses have become more inclusive, I, as a woman, sometimes had to raise my voice—figuratively and literally—just to be heard. I could not afford to be meek or uncertain; I had to be assertive to be taken seriously, something my male counterparts were never required to do. While I was proud of my strength and resilience, it also felt like a constant reminder that women in business still face many obstacles.

Despite all the challenges, the moments of doubt only fuelled my determination. I wanted to prove to them and myself that I was fully capable of understanding every intricate detail—from weaving patterns and fabric quality to negotiating deals and placing orders. When Piharwa's brand started gaining recognition, I knew I had silenced that doubt, not just for them but for every woman who dreams of carving her own path in the business world.

Just when I felt we were settling in and had found our footing, fate intervened in the form of an unforeseen adversary—COVID-19. The pandemic brought the world to a standstill and created uncertainty for the future of businesses, large and small. Yet, amidst the fear and confusion, we found comfort in the realisation that the digital realm offered a lifeline during those troubled times.

With newfound hope and determination, we shifted our focus to our online presence, navigating the unknown waters of e-commerce with resilience and adaptability. Today, with a sense of profound humility and gratitude, I take pride in Piharwa standing tall in the digital sphere, offering our curated collection to patrons far and wide through our online platform, WWW.PIHARWA.COM.

As I look back, I reflect on my journey, filled with challenges and successes, which serves as a reminder of the strength of the human spirit and teamwork. With the three pillars of my business—Retail, Institutional, and E-Commerce—I am ready to face future challenges and opportunities.

- Prakriti Jain

AUTHOR INTRODUCTION

Prakriti Jain is the Founder and Brand Owner of Piharwa, a brand driven by her passion for preserving India's rich handloom heritage. She is committed to empowering women and aims to make Piharwa a globally renowned name in the handwoven textile industry.

Prakriti holds a B. Com from BMCC College, Pune, an MBA in Marketing and Human Resources from the University of Pune, and has completed executive education in Digital Marketing and Analytics from the Indian School of Business. Her professional journey includes over 3.5 years of corporate experience at Cummins India Ltd, followed by a key role at AB Leasing & Finance Ltd, where she honed her human resources and leadership skills. In 2011, she entered the retail sector, which led to the launch of Piharwa in 2017, specializing in handloom, silk, and handcrafted luxury items.

In addition to her entrepreneurial pursuits, Prakriti has held leadership roles with CII YI and the Entrepreneurs Organization (EO), which has contributed to her strong business acumen. Born in Jaipur and having lived in various cities, she brings a deep understanding of India's diverse cultural landscape to her work.

Prakriti is always open to connecting and collaborating with those who share her vision of promoting Indian craftsmanship globally.

Connect with Prakriti, Piharwa:

Linktree: https://linktr.ee/jprakriti
Instagram: @jprakriti1508 @piharwa
LinkedIn: www.linkedin.com/in/prakriti-jain-677b5b34
YouTube: www.youtube.com/@piharwabhopal7402

***

The Spark of Inspiration

Soundarya Lahari Vedula
Founder, Mahasvana

It all began on an unassuming evening in Kuwait, under a starlit sky that gave no hint of the transformative experience about to unfold. The cultural organisation that had invited me to speak was held in high esteem, and the auditorium was an architectural marvel, magnifying the gravity of the occasion. As I made my way onto the stage, the soft murmur of the assembled crowd tapered into hushed anticipation, signalling that this was no ordinary gathering. I was there to share not just another speech but a personal saga of my unyielding quest for excellence.

Growing up, my life was characterised by an insatiable drive for achievement. Whether it was excelling in academics, captivating audiences with my dance performances, or clinching trophies at public speaking competitions, the journey was relentless. However, the shiny facade of success often masked the rigorous discipline and intense training behind it. That evening, I peeled back the curtain to reveal the tough realities—the discipline, the sacrifices, and the almost fanatical dedication required to pursue such goals. I laid bare the not-so-glamorous truths about the path to success, inviting the audience to see the real person behind the accolades.

As I recounted the myriad challenges I had faced, nods of understanding rippled through the audience. They recognised the universal struggle against burnout, the battle with self-doubt, and the resilience needed to overcome them. The real turning point of the evening came during the Q&A session when a young woman raised a question that cut to the heart of the matter: "How do you keep pushing, even when everything feels impossible?" Her voice, laced with a mix of frustration and hope, mirrored many of the internal battles I had once faced.

The auditorium, filled with young faces looking for direction, became a mirror reflecting my own past uncertainties. In responding, I drew upon my deepest reserves of honesty, sharing stories of nights filled with fear, moments brimming with frustration, and the dawn of new days that brought renewed determination. The dialogue that followed transcended typical Q&A exchanges; it turned into a profound sharing of experiences and vulnerabilities, connecting on a deeply emotional level.

As the evening concluded, the light of the insights shared was palpable. The feedback was overwhelming—many attendees spoke of a pervasive lack of motivation among their peers, confirming my growing realisation that this struggle is generational. The seeds for Mahasvana, a platform aimed at reigniting motivation, were sown right there in that auditorium, fuelled by the urgent needs reflected in the eyes of hundreds of young individuals.

This unforgettable night deepened my understanding of my mission. It was not just about sharing strategies for success; it was about fostering a community of support and encouragement, proving that no one should face their challenges alone. This experience underscored the vital need for a beacon of hope, and I was determined to light that beacon for others. Inspired by this profound realisation, I set out to create Mahasvana, not just as a platform but as a beacon of hope for those seeking direction and motivation in their lives.

Unveiling Mahasvana

The very name "Mahasvana," meaning "Great Sound" in Sanskrit, aptly captures the essence of my initiative. Sound, recognised since ancient times as a potent, enlightening, and stimulating medium for transmitting knowledge, fascinates and drives this venture forward. Thus, through Mahasvana, I am dedicated to harnessing the profound art of sound science, using my voice to spark new waves of enlightenment and excitement.

In creating Mahasvana, I noticed a gap between traditional motivational advice and the real-life challenges faced by today's youth. Insights from successful figures often seem disconnected from the everyday realities of young people. This critical insight paved the way for the foundation of Mahasvana—a platform where motivational guidance is not merely dispensed from an elevated position but is deeply rooted in relatable, real-life experiences. Having recently transitioned from student life myself, I possess a profound understanding of the dilemmas, ambitions, and psyche of today's youth. This personal connection ensures that the counsel provided at Mahasvana resonates profoundly with my audience, making it uniquely impactful.

At Mahasvana, I view motivation not merely as a transient emotion but as a continuous journey—one that commences with understanding, progresses through inspiration, and culminates in actionable change. This comprehensive and holistic approach distinguishes Mahasvana, positioning it not just as a source of motivation but as a powerful catalyst for life-altering transformation among our students.

The foundation of Mahasvana, laid with such care and intention, was ready. However, as with any great endeavour, the true test comes not in the dreaming but in the doing. It was time to bring Mahasvana from the realm of ideas into the tangible, often unpredictable world of reality.

Navigating the Storm

While the conceptual foundation of Mahasvana was inspired by the profound potential of sound to enact change, the journey to realise this vision involved significant challenges.

Each day, driven by purpose, I invested countless hours into creating content, designing a website, and tackling technical complexities. Despite this clarity, the onset of each day brought with it not just opportunities but an undercurrent of stress that seemed to intensify as the hours passed. The mornings began with optimism, but by afternoon, the enormity of my tasks would often morph into a tangible tension that clouded my thoughts and tightened around my chest. This stress was a relentless companion, whispering doubts and amplifying fears about the future of my endeavours. The weight of creating something meaningful from scratch, the pressure to succeed, and the solitude of the journey often left me overwhelmed. There were moments when I sat in my office, surrounded by plans and prototypes, feeling utterly alone in my struggle. The excitement that sparked my mornings frequently faded into a cocktail of anxiety and exhaustion by dusk.

Amidst these challenging times, I found an unexpected ally in my daily dance practice. Every morning, before the sun rose too high, I devoted at least thirty minutes to dance. This routine was not just a physical activity but a sacred ritual that allowed me to connect deeply with myself beyond the entrepreneurial identity I was crafting. Dance became my moving meditation, my way of shedding the layers of stress that accumulated each day. As I moved to the rhythms that I knew by heart, my home studio transformed into a space of freedom and creativity. Here, there were no deadlines, no expectations, no fears of failure. The physical motions helped dissolve the tension in my muscles, and the music soothed my frayed nerves. This practice became essential for maintaining both my physical and mental well-being.

Moreover, the discipline of dance instilled a resilience that permeated other aspects of my life. It reminded me that grace under pressure was possible and that every step, no matter how small, was part of a larger dance towards my goals. It taught me to embrace the ebb and flow of my emotions, allowing me to return to my entrepreneurial challenges with renewed vigour and a clearer mind. The morning dance sessions were not just breaks from work; they were vital to managing stress and reconnecting with my initial passion for Mahasvana.

Reinvigorated by my daily dance sessions, I approached the creation of Mahasvana's content and courses with a clear mind and a determined spirit. This next phase required translating the essence of what Mahasvana stood for into engaging, educational material—a task that proved both exhilarating and daunting. Each piece of content, be it a video or a course module, began as a seed of an idea—often sparked by a personal insight or a motivational theory that resonated deeply with me. From there, extensive research followed, where I spent hours gathering real-world examples to make the concepts relatable and engaging for a diverse audience.

Creating the videos as part of the courses was particularly challenging. The goal was to condense complex ideas into shorter, digestible segments that maintained the viewer's interest throughout. This required a careful balancing act—simplifying the content without diluting its impact and ensuring each video was packed with value. The filming process itself was a trial of patience and learning; I would often find myself shooting a video, reviewing it, and realising it did not convey the message as powerfully as I intended. This led to multiple reshoots—sometimes four to five times for a single video—each iteration guided by a critical self-review until my heart confirmed, "This is correct." One particular instance stands out—a video I created on the importance of hard work. Initially, I was confident in the script; it was concise and informative, structured around what I thought was a compelling real-world example. However, upon reviewing the footage, a sinking feeling took hold. The example, which had seemed persuasive on paper, did not translate with the conviction and impact I had hoped for on screen. Driven by a commitment to authenticity and effectiveness, I dove back into research. I sifted through articles, books, and studies, searching for a narrative that would not only illustrate hard work but would also ignite a spark in the viewers. After hours of this iterative process, I finally found a story that felt right—a tale of an entrepreneur who overcame tremendous odds through sheer mental fortitude. Energised, I reshot the video, this time with a narrative that I believed could truly inspire.

Sharing these preliminary versions with my mentors brought another layer of complexity. Their feedback provided invaluable perspectives and suggestions that enhanced the content's delivery. Each piece of advice led to further revisions and reshoots, making the iterative process emotionally taxing but ultimately rewarding. The desire to perfect each piece of content often led to long nights and early mornings filled with editing and re-editing until every segment of the video felt precise and impactful.

Moreover, despite being confident in my content, delivering it effectively on camera was a new skill I had to cultivate. There was a significant learning curve, from mastering the technical aspects of filming to developing a comfortable on-camera presence. Slowly, I began to connect with my audience through the lens, a crucial skill for ensuring the quality and impact of the courses. This meticulous approach to content creation and delivery taught me invaluable lessons about persistence, attention to detail, and the importance of resonating with the audience on an emotional level.

As I honed my skills in content creation and delivery, the challenges of Mahasvana's development extended beyond video production. The development of Mahasvana's website and its marketing strategy presented their own sets of challenges. Far removed from the glitzy, quick-fix appeal of startup pitches on popular shows like "Shark Tank," the actual process was a gritty and relentless grind that spanned every conceivable aspect of starting and growing a business. Building a user-friendly, aesthetically pleasing online platform took countless hours of collaboration with designers and IT specialists. Marketing, too, was a steep learning curve—crafting messages that resonated with potential participants and converting interest into engagement required a blend of creativity and analytical skills. Each of these elements demanded a harmonious blend of vision and execution, testing my patience and perseverance.

Despite these hurdles, my dedication never wavered. The process, though more demanding and time-consuming than I had ever anticipated, was driven by a commitment to making Mahasvana not just a vision but a reality. After months of relentless work, adapting strategies, and overcoming setbacks, Mahasvana was finally ready to launch. The satisfaction of overcoming these challenges was profound, marking the beginning of a new chapter in my journey and the lives of those Mahasvana would touch.

Baby Steps: From Struggles to Success

Despite the triumph of launching Mahasvana, the journey didn't go as smoothly as anticipated. The early days post-launch were filled with anticipation and anxiety. To attract customers, I threw myself into a series of aggressive outreach efforts. I delivered public pitches at local seminars, hosted informative sessions in gated communities, and participated in numerous networking events, hoping to spark interest and gain traction. Yet, despite these efforts, the response was dishearteningly tepid. Weeks passed without a single sign-up, testing my resolve and pushing me to question the appeal and impact of my platform. Meanwhile, I also faced criticism from various quarters—friends, potential customers, and casual observers alike questioned the viability and value of paying for motivational courses. Comments that dismissed the courses as unnecessary or a waste of time were deeply hurtful, casting doubt on my vision and the core mission of Mahasvana. These criticisms went beyond simple scepticism about the business model; they felt like direct challenges to my belief in the transformative power of motivation and self-improvement.

Dealing with such scepticism was emotionally taxing. Every doubt or negative comment from someone whose opinion I valued felt like a personal indictment of my choices and vision. There were nights filled with introspection and self-doubt, where I questioned the sanity of my endeavour and whether there truly was a demand for what Mahasvana offered. This barrage of negativity often made the entrepreneurial journey feel isolating and lonely.

However, during these low points, the importance of a strong support network became unmistakably clear. My husband was an unwavering pillar of strength, providing emotional backing and critical business insights that were invaluable. Our strategy sessions together helped dispel doubts and made me refocus on the mission ahead. My parents constantly encouraged me, reinforcing their faith in my capabilities, which was crucial during those challenging times. My uncle contributed his expertise, suggesting ways to enhance the educational quality and engagement of my content.

Four weeks after going live, however, the moment I had been tirelessly working towards finally arrived. I secured my first customer. The rush of emotions was overwhelming; a mix of relief, joy, and a deep sense of validation flooded through me. It felt incredible, surreal even, to realise that what I had envisioned and built was starting to make a difference to someone out there. This initial sign-up was more than just a business transaction; it was a signal that Mahasvana had potential, that my voice could reach and impact others, and, most importantly, that the challenges and uncertainties were beginning to bear fruit. The experience of gaining that first customer reinvigorated my spirit and reaffirmed my commitment to Mahasvana. It was a poignant reminder that success often starts small and that perseverance is key. With renewed energy, I began to refine my approach, taking the lessons learned from those silent initial days to enhance our outreach and engagement strategies. This first success story was just the beginning, but it was a vital step that paved the way for many more to come.

Soon, Mahasvana started to stabilise and grow in customer count. Testimonials from users who reported genuine, positive changes in their lives validated our efforts and mission. These stories are not just professional affirmations of Mahasvana's business model; they are personal victories over the tide of scepticism that had once seemed insurmountable.

This journey taught me that entrepreneurship is as much about personal resilience and belief as it is about business acumen. As Mahasvana continues to expand and reach a new audience, the scars from those early criticisms serve not as wounds but as reminders of the resilience required to transform a dream into reality. Each step forward takes me further from the echoes of doubt, moving even closer to a world where motivation and personal growth are not just sought after but recognised as essential for everyone. Emboldened by these lessons and the expanding impact of our work, the scope of Mahasvana is set to broaden even further.

Envisioning the Future of Mahasvana

As Mahasvana's journey unfolds, my vision for its future continues to expand and evolve. What began as a platform to rekindle motivation among the youth has grown into a much broader mission. My aspiration is to make Mahasvana a comprehensive hub—a one-stop destination that caters to diverse needs and challenges. Whether it is a student grappling with academic pressure, a housewife seeking to rediscover her purpose, or an employee striving for balance amidst corporate chaos, I want to be there for them at all times. My goal is to offer not just motivation but also practical tools for developing one's personality, fostering mental peace, and finding joy and contentment in everyday life.

To achieve this, I plan to broaden the scope of Mahasvana's offerings. My focus is on expanding the platform's offerings to include live webinars and one-on-one sessions. These additions will provide real-time interaction and personalised guidance, enhancing the learning experience. By incorporating diverse formats and personalised interactions, I aim to deepen the connection between participants and the motivational content.

Furthermore, recognising the diverse linguistic and cultural tapestry of our global audience, I plan to dissipate my content in various local languages, making Mahasvana more inclusive and accessible to a global audience and fostering a broader and more diverse community. By doing so, I aim to resonate with a broader audience, ensuring that language is not a barrier to accessing high-quality motivational resources.

The future I envision for Mahasvana is ambitious yet grounded in the successes I have already witnessed. As Mahasvana grows, I will continually adapt it to meet the evolving needs of its community, always striving to offer more than just motivation.

Thus, I want to make Mahasvana a sound of transformation that echoes in every ear that listens and in every heart that seeks change. With each step forward, I want to craft a legacy of empowerment and transformation that will resonate for generations to come.

As I look back on the roads I have travelled and forward to the paths yet to be explored, I understand that my journey is far from over.

Echoes of a Beginning

In the spirit of Mahasvana I find this to be not just a conclusion but a perpetual beginning. This book, this journey—it is not just a recounting of steps taken; it is an ongoing dialogue with every soul it touches, a continuous challenge to rise, to reflect, and to resonate with purpose.

I have taken the first steps—bold, unsteady, exhilarating steps—towards a vision that seeks to transform not just individuals but generations. The road has been anything but predictable, littered with both triumphs and trials, each teaching me more about the world and myself than I had ever anticipated.

In the spirit of Mahasvana, let us move forward, not just with hope but also with strong conviction. Embrace the uncertainty, relish the unknown, and trust in the journey. The sound of transformation is calling. How will you answer?

- Soundarya Lahari Vedula

~~~
~~~

AUTHOR INTRODUCTION

Soundarya Lahari Vedula is a prominent corporate strategist and corporate lawyer renowned for her educational and professional accomplishments. She earned her B.A. LL.B. (Hons.) degree in 2018 from the prestigious National Law Institute University, Bhopal, securing five gold medals for her stellar academic performance. She continued her academic pursuit with a Master's in International Business from the University of New South Wales, Sydney, where she graduated in 2021, receiving both the Dean's List recognition and an Academic Excellence Award. Her career has spanned various countries, including India, Australia, and Germany, with significant roles at top-tier companies.

Soundarya is also a passionate Kuchipudi dancer and has graced stages worldwide, including the famed Nadaneerajanam in Tirupati. Committed to social betterment, she supports various NGOs and employs her deep understanding of societal challenges in her volunteer work. Soundarya is the visionary founder of Mahasvana—a platform dedicated to guiding young minds through motivational and practical advice to navigate life's challenges, making her a multifaceted leader shaping both business and the community.

Connect with Soundarya Lahari Vedula, Mahasvana:

Webpage: www.mahasvana.com
YouTube: www.youtube.com/@mahasvanamotivation
LinkedIn: www.linkedin.com/in/soundarya-lahari
Instagram: soundarya_lahari456
Facebook: www.facebook.com/soundarya.lahari.5

OccuPassion: Merging Passion with Profession for a Purposeful Life

Nethra S
Co-Founder, Prachitee Experiential School

May 2023

I chose red for the big day, a brand-new salwar suit! I had a busy few days before and had not slept well the previous night, but I was all excited and happy! The campus was decorated in the front with coconut and mango leaves and fresh flowers. Oh yes, I am talking about the day my dream turned into reality: the inauguration of my preschool, Prachitee Experiential School.

1980's

As a child, I would wrap a dupatta around myself, with a stick in hand, lay a few books on the ground, and start my role as a teacher. Becoming a teacher was my childhood passion. But my grandfather had set a goal for me, which my father had to make sure I fulfilled. I was growing up in a family where I was never asked about my choices, and I did not have a say in them either.

21st Century

Since my grandfather's dream was to see me become a doctor, I had to take Science as my subject in college. I scored quite well in the second pre-university exams but my CET ranking for medical entrance did not fetch me a medical seat in Bangalore. Since my father was not keen on sending me away from home, he said the only other thing I should do is become an Engineer, a Software Engineer! Oh No! Computers were the subject I had hated most since high school, and here I was in a situation where I could not say no but just do what I was told.

In four years, I graduated as a Computer Science Engineer with Distinction. But that did not get me a job in a software company immediately after I graduated. For almost nine months after graduating, I was looking for a job, applying on company websites and job sites, and personally visiting companies to hand over my resume. I gave a couple of tests and interviews but in vain. At this point, my father's new goal was that I must land a job in Infosys. I worked hard, cleared the entrance exam, and was called for the HR interview, but I got nervous and did not pass it. I had to wait for nine months to reapply at Infosys. My job hunt continued.

At this point in my life, the person who helped me kickstart my career is my Uncle Pavan Kumar. I am greatly indebted to him as he helped me get a job in a firm named Edurite Technologies that was headed by his friend. I joined as a software tester, and the job interested me as I did not have to do any coding (which I hated). I only had to test and find flaws in the content and design of the educational videos that the company produced. During this time, as the nine-month gap of reapplying to Infosys came to a close, I applied again and cleared the entrance exam. I was called for the interview; this time, I was well-prepared and determined to crack it. I continued to work as a tester while eagerly awaiting the result of the interview. I had to clear it this time; otherwise, my father would not be pleased.

One fine day, I received an email from Infosys stating that I was selected for the job and had to report to Mysore in a month. I was happy I got a job at Infosys and achieved the goal set for me by my father. From there began my journey of working for a multinational company, a job I was not satisfied with, yet I continued on this journey for over two years until wedding bells rang in my life.

My husband is one of the greatest blessings of my life. Having married a supportive, wise, and understanding person made me realise that I no longer needed to fulfil the dreams of others but that it was time to live my own. Very soon he figured out how dissatisfied I was with my job and supported me when I made the decision to quit my job and join him on his onsite trip to the UK. In less than eight months, we returned to India. Due to the recession, my husband had to return to his base branch, whereas now I was left with no job and was subject to societal pressures.

A woman finds herself under scrutiny and judgment regardless of her choice due to deeply ingrained societal norms and gender biases. When a woman pursues a career, she is often labelled as ambitious or selfish and questioned why she is not planning to start a family yet. If she has, then it is assumed that she is not taking good care of her family. Conversely, women who choose to stay at home and take care of their families are judged as being dependent on their partners or lacking ambition.

I decided never to return to IT and started looking for a Lecturer job in engineering colleges to pursue my passion for teaching. Many colleges denied my application for lecturer as I did not have an MTech degree. My job hunt for a lecturer post continued.

Reading my journey till now, you must think that there was one villain in my life, my father, who never gave me a choice and had full control of my life. Can parents ever be villains? Dads are called superheroes, right? Whatever decisions he made in my life shaped me in different ways and made me what I am today. Though I have some complaints, I am also grateful for everything he has done for me. Eventually, he understood where I was headed and was ever-ready to help me achieve my goals.

Thankfully, my dad supported me during my search for the lecturer post and, with a reference from his friend, helped me get a job in an Engineering college. Realising that my BTech degree would not help me grow in that career choice, I started preparing for the MTech entrance exams. While I continued to prepare for exams, I also enjoyed my role as a lecturer in the college, which lasted for a year. Destiny had different plans for me. I had taken my entrance exams and was awaiting results, and at the same time, I conceived. Heeding the doctor's advice to take bed rest during the first trimester of my pregnancy, I resigned from my job and was resting at home. MTech results were announced, and I scored a pretty good ranking, but I could not travel to Belgaum for the seat selection process. I thought I would take a break from everything for the sake of the baby. In less than three months of conceiving, I had a miscarriage! I was in the middle of nowhere, having resigned from my lecturer job and also missed my chance in the seat selection process for the MTech course.

I was going through a very difficult phase at this time: depressed, having lost my baby and also the job, and being subjected to societal pressures yet again. I stood strong with the support of my husband and parents; they have been the strongest pillars of strength in my life, always by my side, no matter what.

Well, I had one more person by my side—guess who? God. As they say, God always has a plan; trust his plan. I also believe that everything that happens is ultimately for the good. Just when I was feeling lost and unsure of what to do, an onsite offer landed in my husband's lap once again. We decided to pursue this and this time for a long term. We packed our bags and flew far away, away from all the societal pressures.

Three years of my stay in London was wonderful. I spent most of my days exploring the place, reading books at the local library, and a little bit of travelling. My daughter was born there, and I got busy with her. When I was eight months pregnant with my daughter, an incident happened that changed my decision to stay longer in the UK. I was robbed. And my mother, who was visiting me, was hurt in the process, trying to help me. This incident shocked me and my family. So, soon after my daughter turned one, we decided to move back to India. That would also allow her to grow amongst family, with grandparents and cousins.

After my daughter was born, the first three years passed in nurturing her and caring for her. I was a homemaker, spent ample time with her, and made some wonderful memories. She started her schooling when she was three and I got some free time during the first half of the day. I did not want to pursue a job at that time as I wanted to be there for her when she returned home from school and spend time with her. While I was on the lookout for ways to keep myself engaged, I came across an NGO named Acharyas for a Better Community that was working towards uplifting Government schools.

I approached and joined the team and started volunteering in government schools in the area while my daughter was at preschool. I would volunteer one hour a day teaching English language to young children at the government school. I was also a part of the team that conducted sports events, donation drives, and other volunteering activities. I thoroughly enjoyed interacting with and teaching young children and built a very good bond with them. This volunteering journey continued for three years until my daughter started primary school. She was away from home for almost eight hours, and I had more time for myself. And these three years of volunteering had knocked on the doors of my childhood dream yet again: becoming an Educator! Pursuing my passion and making it not just an occupation, but what I believe is an 'Occu-Passion'!

Going back as a lecturer in Engineering colleges was not feasible for me because of the late working hours. Also, the time I spent with young children made me realise that I should work with them as I enjoyed it. I started looking for work in schools close to my residence so that I could get home in time for when my daughter returned from school. After visiting a few schools and a couple of interviews, I was finally selected by a school diagonally opposite my home! How lucky was I! Or should I say God had a plan!

And from there, my journey as a preschool teacher started. Podar Jumbo Kids Whitefield branch has taught me some wonderful lessons. My life took a big turn in this organisation thanks to Swapnil, who has been my Mentor since then. I learned a lot during my tenure here and grew as an Educator.

During my time here, I was sent for a three-day training on Developmental Play, and this course literally transformed my life. It helped me understand why play is important, the developmental milestones in children, how to make learning fun for children, and much more. After this, my way of handling children, understanding their needs, and connecting with them—everything changed for the better. I was recognised as one of the best teachers, and there was a point when parents would ask if their child would have me as their class teacher the upcoming year.

I built a good bond with the Parents and children. Till date, parents of children I previously taught are in touch with me and share updates on their children's lives. They believe that I was a great mentor and will continue to be. They seek advice and remember me during their good and bad times. They believe that, along with the organisation, I played a crucial role in laying a strong foundation for their child's educational journey. This assures me that I have truly made a difference in the lives of young children.

These three years truly changed my life. The way I understood children, how I dealt with them, how I looked at my daughter's developmental milestones, and how I formed a connection not only with my students in school but also with my daughter. I grew as an educator and as a parent, making a difference in the lives of the children who were under my care. Not only the organisation but even parents were extremely impressed with my work. Three years in this organisation was a great learning experience for me.

2022

Just about when the COVID period and all the online classes ended, and school was to open for children, I was waiting to meet with Swapnil to discuss about my role for the upcoming year. But that meeting was a sweet surprise for me as she did not talk about my role for the upcoming year but proposed a partnership in the new project that she was planning to start.

It was an offer I could not decline as starting something on my own was something I had given a thought about, but not very seriously. Humbly, I accepted the offer to partner and start a preschool that would be different from other preschools in the way children learn. This excited me as I always wanted to make a difference in the lives of children, make an impact, and be different from others. My designation sounded very exciting to me, 'Co-Founder & Head of Child Development and Community Outreach', and my roles and responsibilities were interesting too – curriculum development and successful implementation of the same, Teacher training, and Community Building.

We were a team of three. We started researching and working on various aspects of the school - Curriculum, infrastructure, resources, etc. It was challenging yet exciting to build something from scratch. I received immense support from my husband Jagadeesh and daughter Deetya during this time. They have stood by me, understood my scope of work, and have been very supportive.

After a year of hard work, finally, the campus was all set to open on May 12, 2023! I chose red for the big day, a brand-new salwar suit.

Present

Prachitee is an innovative preschool, one of its kind, in Whitefield, Bangalore. It is a project-based experiential school that focuses on hands-on learning. Our in-house curriculum, child-centred learning, and unique approach make us stand out from the rest. Prachitee has successfully completed one academic year, and it has been two years for me on this Entrepreneurial journey since its inception. Entrepreneurship has been a thrilling experience, a roller coaster ride with a lot of ups and downs. The ups have instilled confidence and motivation for me to do better, and the downs have been great learnings.

From working at an 8-3 job as a teacher and being able to balance work and home, the transition to being an entrepreneur was challenging for me. As an entrepreneur setting up my business from scratch, time management and balancing work and personal life were one of the biggest challenges. I cannot thank my family enough for the support given. They understood that I now wear many hats and have multiple things to manage, which can sometimes lead to extended hours. My business partners have been very supportive and understanding too; our teamwork and sharing of responsibilities have made things much easier for all of us.

Prachitee is a new brand, and it is very important for us to build a brand identity. Since we inaugurated mid-May, a crucial time when admissions are in progress in all the schools, the start of the first year was quite challenging. Just a week away from the beginning of the academic year, we only had a handful of admissions. But slowly, word spread, and today, our admissions are almost 10-fold.

Prachitee is growing, and watching this gives me a sense of pride. Parents have seen the quality education and the nurturing environment we offer and are talking about us in the community. Parents have been a huge support in the first year, trusting and having confidence in us. They feel that Prachitee is a second home to their child as we offer a safe, comfortable, and nurturing space for children. Some other very positive feedback we received is that Prachitee focuses on the holistic development of the child and that children are given many opportunities and wonderful experiences to explore and learn.

A personal and best feedback that I personally received from a parent is that I am a God-sent angel in the life of their child. I was overwhelmed to see this caption for a picture of me with the child on the parent's WhatsApp status.

When the news of Prachitee was out, parents of my previous students messaged me asking if we were open for higher grades as well, as without a second thought, they would enrol their child in my school.

I believe that learning is a continuous process, and I am always ready to learn and grow from my past and present experiences.

My vision for Prachitee is that it soars to great heights. I want people to know the school by the impact it is having on the lives of young children and the difference the school is making in their lives, making learning not a boring experience but a fun experience.

The first year of successfully running the preschool has instilled in me the confidence that dreams can be turned into reality. My dream for Prachitee is that it grows and multiplies and wins laurels. In this journey, I also want to grow as an Edupreneur, make progress, and be a role model for many.

I hope my entrepreneurial journey inspires many to do what they are most passionate about. Unlike me, stand up for what you really want to do from the start, and sooner or later, you will soar to great heights.

I end this by thanking all the people who have supported me and stood by me in this journey.

- Nethra S

~~~
~~~

AUTHOR INTRODUCTION

"It's a beautiful thing when a career and passion come together." This resonates well with Nethra as she quit her job as an IT professional to pursue her childhood dream of becoming an Educator. She has an engineering degree in computer science and began her teaching career as a lecturer in an Engineering college. Later on, during her time volunteering in government schools teaching 5–6-year-olds, she found herself inclined to work with young children and joined a preschool where she grew as an Educator. She is a highly energetic and passionate professional who takes pride in being an Educator and focuses on developing lifelong learners. She gets immense satisfaction in contributing to the community and making a difference in the lives of children. She Co-Founded Prachitee Experiential School with a vision to Connect, Ignite & Inspire.

Connect with Nethra S, Prachitee Experiential School:

Webpage: www.prachitee.com
Email: prachiteeschool@gmail.com
LinkedIn: www.linkedin.com/in/nethra-s-7ba40317b
Instagram: @ignitingminds.nethra @prachitee_education
Facebook: www.facebook.com/ProjectBasedExperientialLearning

Grit and Grace: My Entrepreneurial Odyssey

Bhagyashri Mhatre
Founder, Food Monk Consultants LLP

It was a usual workday. I was checking my emails and taking work updates from my staff when the phone rang. I answered it hesitatingly, as it was an international number. The lady on the other side spoke in a soft tone, "Hi, is this Bhagyashri? From Food Monk Consultants?" I said, "Oh yes, Bhagyashri here; how can I help you?" And the conversation started. It was the first international inquiry for my business. What an exciting moment!

I was excited while trying to remain calm. The lady who called me was the director of a company in the Netherlands, Europe, and wanted to launch our Indian products in RTE form. She was looking for a consultant in India to develop their products and to handhold them until the products launched. I was extremely happy and immediately shared the news with my staff. While going through my company's web profile, I realised how far I had come in the last 4-5 years.

Once a shy but bright student, I had never thought of myself as this version. Yes, I had dreamed of starting something of my own since studying for my food technology course. I was often asked how I decided to pursue a B.Tech. in Food Technology as a course. The fact is that it just happened by chance. Honestly, I didn't even know what food technology was. One of my uncle's students enrolled in Food Technology and told him it was a really good course for girls. I was completely clueless. All I knew was that I didn't want to study medicine or pursue computer engineering. Oh, it was such a craze back in 2001!

At that point, I was truly unaware that this line of education and my degree in Food Technology would one day become my identity. In 2005, I successfully completed my B. Tech degree with a distinction. This is when the real struggle to find a suitable job began. Soon, I got lucky and was selected for a job at Asia's biggest fruit processing company, Jain Irrigation System LTD. At the age of 23, I was the first female employee working as a Food Technologist on their production floor. This was the first time I saw all the big machines, and needless to say, I was in awe. We had studied about those machines, but it was all in theory. I realised the stark difference between theory and practically seeing those machines.

I was exposed to all the departments, such as quality check, quality control, R&D, production, ISO certifications, and audits. I could experience and do all the work because of our boss, Mr. Deshpande, who believed in women's power. He always used to say - "Women make the best managers." I was also fortunate to work under the guidance of Mr. Patil as my immediate boss. There were more than 25 male employees working on the production floor in middle management roles. They all supported me, cared for me, taught me, and made my experience better. Those three-plus years created a base of knowledge & experience for me.

Post that, I shifted to Pune, where I had to change my line of work as companies were hesitant to hire a female employee in the production department. So, I started working as an Entrepreneurship Development Trainer for the food processing Industry. That job gave me new horizons. I was introduced to the whole new world of entrepreneurship. Not only was I learning by myself, but I was teaching other people too.

That job gave me many things, most importantly, my identity in a new city. In 2010, I found myself as a small fish in a huge pond, and today, in 2024, I have gained a name, respect, and reputation due to my work. I am eternally grateful to the people who held my hand during my initial days in Pune.

I had always wanted to do something of my own, and this particular job pushed me closer to entrepreneurship. Once I got married and settled in Pune, we both used to share a dream of having our own business, most likely a restaurant business. And, somehow, an opportunity came through one of my friends. We gave it a thought, checked the details, and finalised the deal with the restaurant's owners. We were delighted with the deal we had gotten. I was passionate and excited to run that restaurant. So I quit my job and started working full-time at our restaurant with my husband.

Everything was good until demonetisation happened, and we almost lost the business that we had in our hands. We were emotionally attached to the business and were not ready to accept that it was not working. Eventually, we had to make the difficult decision of quitting our dream. One can pretend everything is fine, but the money doesn't lie. We had made losses and our debt was increasing. This was my second business that failed despite four years of hard work and dedication. Of course, we learned a big lesson from this failure. Oh, you must be wondering why I haven't mentioned my first business, which also failed. Since my college days, I have been fascinated with designer premium chocolates. Before entering the restaurant business, I ran a part-time chocolate business. I did a two-day course and thought, "Now, I am a chocolatier, and I can start my business." But I was completely wrong. I did not do a market study or make any plans for sales and marketing. I had to go through this experience and fail to learn and understand this. This was also a significant loss of hard work, time, energy and a substantial financial setback.

So, this is how by the year 2015, I was carrying a huge burden of these failures. I couldn't sleep at night. We were going through a financial crisis. Hence, I decided to go back to my industry and search for a job. Due to the long break from my previous jobs, I had to accept a new position with a salary of 25,000 per month despite having over nine years of work experience. This job required me to learn new technologies, market treads, etc. And I did it. After that, I joined another company with a good salary of around 75,000 per month. It gave me good relief on the home front. This happiness didn't last for long. Sadly, for some reason, I had to leave that job.

I was going through some medical issues, and doctors had advised me to take a break. I went through various treatments for almost a year, sitting idle at home while consuming medicines. This used to disturb me a lot. I used to see my friends who were doing really well in their careers. And what was I doing? Nothing. Once again, I started searching for a middle management-level job. I received calls from HR departments and was even called for interviews. Despite performing well, not a single company selected me. I had created profiles on Naukri, Shine, and other platforms, but still, no luck.

Meanwhile, my brother introduced me to someone who was planning to launch a few food products in the RTE/RTC category. This person was working as a director of the company and wanted someone to take care of his product development work and other related work until the product launch. I was a bit sceptical at first as I was not confident enough that I would be able to do the work. But, I did say yes and again started working with a 25,000 Rs per month retainer ship fee. At times, I used to think this figure of 25,000 would never leave me. While others were making lakhs of rupees, it often disturbed me. Nevertheless, I continued working, as it was the only thing I could do. That was the 1st break I got to work as a freelance consultant.

While I was still searching for good jobs, one incident became a crucial moment in deciding my next step. A company that I considered to be my dream company called me for an interview for the third time in the span of two years and then rejected me again. The interviewer was significantly younger than me, and it hurt me deeply. That day, I decided, 'Job mangne wale nahi, Job dene wale banenge,' meaning I'll become the one who provides employment to others, not the other way around. It was the turning point of my life that changed something within me. I could sense that something had ignited within me.

I was still working on only one project at that time, and I gave it my heart and soul. I did everything to turn it into a successful product launch. At the same time, I was not happy with the work-from-home scenario. To get the feel of an office, I moved a table with my laptop and some stationery to our guest room and started treating it as my office. I travelled to a few new places during this period for my project. I updated my status and bio on LinkedIn, stating, "I have started working full-time as a consultant." A lot of people congratulated me, and it did increase my confidence. Slowly, I started getting new inquiries. Before this, I did not have any experience in sales. I used to get nervous while talking to people and would get scared when quoting my fee, even if it was just 35,000 Rs. I used to think, 'Why will they pay me? Ye thoda jyada to nahi ho raha hai?' (Isn't it too much?). I started researching other companies but failed to understand their fee structure. I started attending domestic and international exhibitions to enhance my knowledge about the latest trends. Just when I began to feel that I had found my track, COVID happened, and again, everything stopped suddenly. Unable to move out of our houses, we all felt helpless during this time. Inquiries stopped, and clients denied advance as promised, as no one was sure what would happen next. It was an extremely difficult time for all of us, and somehow, we survived those two years. We are bound to feel hopeless and helpless when there is no income source and no guarantee of the future as well.

I somehow managed to get myself out of the comfort as well as the discomfort zone. I started planning things. I started interacting with people and collaborated with a few other companies who could perhaps help me get new clients. I hired a low-budget social media marketing agency and started promoting various webinars on social media. Though the fee was only 99 Rs for the webinar, we had to struggle a lot even to get 30 participants. But I kept doing it. I had a plan in my mind. You may find it hard to believe, but during the Covid period, I became a home chef and a food blogger. One of my close friends suggested it to me, and I took it a bit seriously. I even attended a few blogger tables, reviewed restaurants, and ran in that rat race to get more and more followers.

I could achieve a good number of 5000+ followers, but it was not my core. I stopped going to restaurants to have so-called "free food."

I even started getting irritated with fellow bloggers and their rat race. I started focusing back on my work. I knew I was meant for the food processing industry only. As soon as the lockdown period ended, I started working full-fledged. Networking and learning were happening simultaneously. I got to work on 2-3 other new projects, which was when I hired my 1st employee. I was certain that once I became successful, the majority of my staff would be female. I wanted to create job opportunities specifically for women, ensuring they wouldn't face the challenges I did. It all happened in 2021, and we kept going with a lot of work, client pressure, successes, failures, etc. No matter what, I kept working. Then, I gave my company a good name, again without researching the Ministry of Corporate Affairs site. However, we were fortunate enough to get a domain name for our website. I hired a team to build my website and did a lot of research on what the website should include and how it should look. And then, finally, one fine day, my website www.foodmonkconsultant.com was live. I was overwhelmingly happy. We got an identity in the digital world. You can simply ask people to check the website, and it creates a good impression. And with this, our journey on social media and electronic media started.

I increased my staff to four while we were still working from our guest room. If a client asked me for a meeting, I would meet them at the nearest coffee shop. We didn't have an office space to sit and have client meetings. In October 2022, I rented my 1st office, which was a dream come true. And then, it was time for company registration. People found it hard to believe that until then, I was running the company as a proprietor. In 2023, our company got a formal structure in the Ministry of Corporate Affairs. I was fulfilling my dreams one by one, and my responsibilities were also increasing with it.

People started recognising me as the founder of Food Monk Consultants. The last two years have been really great. I was recognised by “Perfect Woman Magazine” as one of the top 30 Perfect Women in business, received the “Pune Udyajok Puraskar Award” in 2023, and was honoured with special recognition by Business Icon as “Navdurga in Business 2023” in Pune. Before all this recognition, I first received a huge surprise by being recognised as a 'Fighter Woman in Business' by an organisation called J4E (Just 4 Entrepreneurs). All this has felt and still sometimes feels overwhelming. I can see and feel the respect in people’s eyes. Previously, people used to wonder what I would do. Now, their perspective has completely changed. My journey has only just begun, and I'm still in the process. I've successfully developed over 50 food products and assisted entrepreneurs in launching them into the market. Of course, my vision is broader, aiming to assist 1000 startups/entrepreneurs by 2032. Currently, I happily employ six people and have connected with over 500 entrepreneurs to date.

It gives us immense satisfaction to make our parents proud of us. I am grateful to my parents, who provided a secure environment, higher education, and the confidence to become independent in all aspects. Family support plays an essential role in all these achievements, and I am fortunate to have my husband beside me every step of the way. Without his strong support, I would not have achieved these things. Significant credit goes to my late grandfather, Mr. Balvantrao Chavan, who shaped our childhood and always encouraged the women in our family to pursue higher education and work independently. He was the best grandfather in the world, and I'm grateful to my uncles & aunts as well, who taught us all the basics in our childhood. Their help and guidance shaped our future, giving us strength, patience, and perseverance. I was lucky to always have my siblings around me, who are the true cheerleaders. My close friends are my support system.

I also attribute a huge part of my success to my hard work. Nothing is possible without a vision combined with hard work. I always give myself a pat on the back and say, 'Shabbas Bhagyashri, you did it and you will rock!' Ma'am Sudha Murty is my idol, and I admire her greatly. She is the perfect example of a businesswoman and a leader. As she says, 'Vision without action is merely a dream, action without vision is merely passing the time, but vision and action together can change the world.

I'm writing the last piece of this story from Hotel W Dubai while enjoying a view of the seashore on one side. I can afford this luxury because of my business, so keep going. Travel around the world, make your people happy, and be proud of yourself.

As I completed this last part, I received an email from NSRCEL IIMB. I have been selected for a prestigious Goldman Sachs 10000 women's Programme, which will be held at IIM Bangalore. I am one step closer to my dreams. Oh, God, I am so overwhelmed with gratitude. I believe strongly in the universe and its law of attraction. This journey and the Universe are going to give me everything I wish for.

- Bhagyashri Mhatre

AUTHOR INTRODUCTION

Bhagyashri Mhatre, a young and dynamic food technologist turned entrepreneur, is the founder of Food Monk Consultants LLP. Bhagyashri completed her B.Tech in Food Technology from UICT, Kaviyatri Bahinabai North Maharashtra University, Jalgaon, Maharashtra. After completing her B.Tech, she began her career with Asia's largest fruit processing company, Jain Irrigation Systems Ltd. Following this, she gained experience with several other organisations. Armed with this experience, she founded her own business, Food Monk Consultants LLP, in Pune, which caters to clients across PAN India.

In her free time, Bhagyashri loves travelling, listening to music, and reading Marathi and English fiction novels.

Connect with Bhagyashri Mhatre, Food Monk Consultants:

Instagram: @foodmonkconsultants @bhagyashripuresoul
LinkedIn: www.linkedin.com/in/ft-bhagyashri-chavan-mhatre-670b7932
www.linkedin.com/company/food-monk-consultants
Facebook: Food Monk Consultants
www.facebook.com/bhagyashri.chavan.58
Website: www.foodmonkconsultant.com

***

I Want to Have it ALL!

Harshada Singh
Founder, Dignity Wealth For You/
Dignity Management Pvt Ltd

In today's era, when times have changed, we see young girls nurturing their minds to be independent and have a career. They want to have an identity of their own. It's not like old times when women used to be homemakers. There is nothing wrong with being a homemaker. In fact, being a homemaker is a lot of work, taking care of the entire family, keeping in mind everyone's favourite things and everyone's necessities, and managing everyone's time. They hardly have any "*ME TIME*." As our generation has transitioned between the eras of being a homemaker and a working woman, a common question women face is, "What happens to my career when I marry?" or "What happens when I become a mother?"

Even today, when a woman is ready to get married, she does ask and has this question in her mind or on her checklist— "Would it be ok for the groom if I continue to work?" "What happens to my career, when we have kids?", and mind you, it is a very important topic that this generation should ask each other for a better understanding and less arguments in the future. Further probe is also required as to "Who would come during and after the pregnancy, to take care of me and the baby?" "Would you be comfortable sending the kids to a daycare?"

When I completed my Specialization in Banking and Finance, I got the opportunity to work at the esteemed bank, Citibank. This is where I met my husband, a gem of a person and a wonderful guy. Truly loving, caring, and extremely supportive. When we decided to plan a family, I quit my job and became a homemaker. Today, it is very important that the husband and wife must earn to have a comfortable lifestyle. Living in a metro city, undoubtedly, it is required.

I am sure every educated woman has heard this, "you are educated, you were such a bright student, you excelled in your class, why are you wasting all of that? Why are you throwing your career away?" Start fresh! Many must have heard, "Now that you are a mother, you have a family; you need to take care of your husband and the baby." Your husband is "WELL TO DO", why do you need to work? "Sweetie, that's how life is", "apana PATANI DHARAM nibhao". Not many care or bother to ask what you really want. I have never really understood, why women have to always be the one to make the choice and be answerable. Why is SHE, the one who is always looked down on? Surprisingly, by another woman. In the midst of all this, I had an unconditionally loving husband who knew my capabilities and asked what I would like to do.

We decided to start a company of our own. Starting from scratch is always difficult, but it is the most wonderful feeling to have something of your own. With a little baby in my hand, I was able to manage a lot because of the happiness and fulfilment that I would be working for myself, and this was something I wanted to do. I wanted to be the best and excel in it. This kept me going! The best thing (I think) we did was we never shared with either of our parents that we were going to start a company. It was almost after 6-8 months that we broke the news to them. Needless to say, it was a shocker for them, but by then, we were done with a lot of work and were mentally prepared for many questions and multiple calls per day. (Believe me, you get many—Q1. Khana Khaya? (Did you eat?) Q2. Business kaisa chal raha hai? (How is the business going?) Q3. Do you need anything? The last one clearly means money for the monthly expenses. Our son Saharsh was not even one year old when we started, so we had two babies, Dignity and Saharsh (priorities are not necessarily in the same order, but they can be; who knows?)

A little back story—When my husband asked me, "What I wanted to do? with a six-month-old baby in my hand, I replied, "I want to do something of my own; I don't want to work for someone else or take a job." That day, after putting Saharsh to sleep, we sat down with hot coffee, "A lot can happen over a coffee" turned out to be the best thing for us. As a mother, I wanted to have enough time for the baby because it is truly important. That's why I left my job. We bring these little angels into the world for our happiness and as per our desire. It is a must that we give them enough time. That's what really matters most to them. I wanted to be there for Saharsh at all times. I know this is a very difficult choice for a woman. The biological clock and the career clock always tick at the same time, and we always have to choose. Choose wisely, be brave and proud, and make peace with what you have chosen.

So, at the time, all we knew was banking, investing, and servicing clients with all their financial needs. So, we decided to start with our wealth management company. The most difficult thing in the entrepreneur's journey is "*STARTING*".

Being an entrepreneur, you have to do everything all by yourself from day one. The best part was with my husband being by my side I had the courage and motivation to move ahead in this journey. You need to have multiple licenses, certifications, and documents in place. The moment you begin, you feel things are so difficult, and various thoughts ponder, and you start thinking: is this whole journey going to be this way? You often have doubts about whether you have chosen and taken the right decision for you or you will have to go back to what you were doing? I remember taking Saharsh to the exam centre, my husband and Saharsh waiting outside for me to complete my exam. Times can be difficult, but your determination makes them less difficult for you. Importantly, these difficult times become a memory for you. Later in life when you think that if you were able to do that, surely you can conquer the next hurdle and move on towards a successful path.

Today, when I see that the Indian Government has made it so convenient for Start-Ups or Gen-Z to take the initiative with a single platform—one window where they can track and get all documentation, necessary licenses, and certifications in one place—

it's a big hurray! The first step in the journey is now easy and smooth.

The Government has been motivating young minds to *start-up* and *stand up* with new ventures and various career options which weren't available ten years ago. C'mon, could you dream of being an influencer? It's a legit career today. A six-figure income on a weekly basis. Isn't that amazing? A gamer? There are competitions for online gaming. It's called E-Sports, played in various countries at the national level. It is brilliant! So much exposure and opportunities for the young ones. Kudos! That we are being progressive about so many things that are happening around us today. The acceptance today from society motivates the ones who are looking for a tiny bit of support. To hold on to that one thought that, "Yes, it can be done, and I am here for a long haul." It is great to see that our Prime Minister talks about vocal for locals, directing the business to the local artisan. Who needs to spend on the advertisement when you have superstar marketing for START UP's, Vocal for Local, STAND UP INDIA, Made in India, etc?

When you decide to start, please remember the reason why you started, and don't depend on anyone. Don't think that he or she will be there to help you out. No, that really doesn't work. You are out and on your own. Your close family and friends will support you but won't buy your services or products. In the majority of cases, as an entrepreneur, I have observed that the family and closest friends like to watch you from a distance as to how you are really doing. Let's say for example, if you are an influencer on a social media platform, your relatives and closest friends are watching you but won't like and definitely won't comment on your post or reel. They think, if they do so, you might get one million followers, or you would be famous overnight. In our case it was different; our family came in full support to avail our services, definitely supported us, and referred us to their friends. That's what we really needed. We did a great job of solving and catering to our extended family's financial well-being.

The second major step is finding the right set of people. Even though you are a One Woman Army, you do need a team, and that, my friend, is difficult to find. You are lucky if you have the right set of people and they are aligned with your mindset, views, and focus as to where you would like to see yourself in the next 5 years. It is a task, but eventually you get there. Your team members are like the pillars of your company. They are there to watch your back while you are out for meetings, taking up calls, while you are busy finding a way ahead to lead the company in the right direction. I am very happy that I have my team members and very thankful to all who have been and are associated with us including my house-help. House help is most important, every time that I step out, I can fully rely on her and be confident that she is there to manage and take care of everything in my absence. Being a woman you have to manage, organize, and build a system in a way where things and household chores are managed and completed even in your absence. Women constantly have to juggle their responsibilities and multiple roles. This develops a habit of multitasking, which is highly beneficial in business. We excel at working under pressure. Haven't we all experienced this? The early morning rush, preparing tiffins for kids and husband, getting the kids ready for school, packing bags, handling projects, and ensuring everyone is well-fed before leaving home.

Third, the most important is what you wish to build? and how you wish to build it. We wanted our company to be built with strong core values where the client is at the centre. We started the financial planning for our clients around these core values. We have seen many companies close down or discontinue their business as there was a lack of value system in their business. We emphasized a lot on the values. In a middle-class family, values are something that our parents are most proud of. We inculcated them in our company and ensured our team members were aligned with these values.

While we were brainstorming names for our company, we wanted to choose something that would be meaningful to everyone.

Upon a lot of thinking and daily discussions, we came up with the name "Dignity Management." The idea behind the name was— in the older times government jobs were seen as white-collar positions with a pension and a constant flow of income. Well, times changed and so did this perception. Younger family members started earning and contributing towards the family's needs and sharing responsibilities. Yet, there remains a sense of guilt in the heart or mind of the family head to be the provider. It's the emotion of dignity—to be the head of the family, the responsible one, the eldest, the provider.

Dignity Management helps people to lead their retired life with Dignity by managing their wealth for them. This is how we came up with the company's name: Dignity Management Private Limited or Dignity Wealth For You, where we work towards the goal of creating a Wealth Corpus for our clientele and providing a solution to many. In today's time, when government jobs don't have the option of pension, or even in private where there is no option for a retirement fund. Dignity Wealth For You has various ways to plan that retirement fund or pension fund for you through Systematic Withdrawal Plans, where you could freely retire without worrying about the funds and continue to be that family head while maintaining the same lifestyle.

We have customized and tailored products for individuals to meet their financial goals, be it education planning for their kids, retirement fund for them and their spouse, their dream car or a vacation, etc.

The Financial Industry is vast, and every product is available for an individual to buy, but is it truly required in their portfolio? and do they really need it is the question we ask ourselves before we recommend? We started evaluating where we could be of help to the investors and how we could make a difference in their lives. We have always tried to protect our clients from a downside. That's what has differentiated us from the rest.

Today, we have clients all over the globe, and we are happy to see that we have brought a change in the way people behave with their finances. There is so much clarity and confidence in our women clients with their money. Women generally take a back seat when there is a discussion about finances and investing. What we do is dig deeper to understand the everyday problems and challenges women face in their day-to-day lives so that we can come up with an appropriate solution that can help them be debt-free and handle money smartly. We explain the financial jargon in the simplest manner so that they are a part of the financial planning.

Women should actively participate in planning their finances well, understanding insurance needs, investment goals, retirement planning, and estate planning for their own good.

There are numerous occasions when you feel a little stretched, in a sandwich situation, when you have a deadline, and your family needs you too. With a supportive and understanding husband, I have never had that problem. It is through teamwork and effort that we are able to manage our clients and company, as a "Team." Being a woman, mother, wife, daughter, and sister, you always have to juggle various responsibilities, but, in the end, it always pays off. Your efforts will always be valued.

The woman I would like to thank is my mother-in-law. She raised a very humble and kind human being. As a mother of a boy, I too, have got this opportunity where we teach them gender equality and a sense of responsibility. You do try to inculcate this in your kids so that our coming generation is a finer version of ourselves, who are better, at understanding another human being. Being Thoughtful.

I have written this chapter so that readers are able to start their journey of being financially independent, irrespective of their situations and scenarios. Remember, there is always a way out; you just have to think in your mind that *YOU CAN*, and thereafter, nothing will stop you. I had a wingman who blew under my wings and helped me fly high. He is always happy to see me happy. Find your wingman. It can be anyone: mother, father, sister, daughter, son, brother or friend. Just one person is required to believe in you, but before that, you have to believe in yourself, that you will make a difference and take charge of your life. Rest all will fall in place. Carve your own path and make your own destiny.

A woman can do anything if she decides to put her mind and efforts into it.
- Harshada Singh

~~~
~~~

AUTHOR INTRODUCTION

Harshada Singh is an accomplished entrepreneur and a Certified Financial Planner dedicated to empowering individuals to make informed financial decisions. Her journey into the world of finance began in childhood when she was captivated by the power of money-making and money management. Fascinated by how financial decisions could shape lives, she pursued her passion, specializing in Banking and Finance and securing a job at Citibank. However, driven by her entrepreneurial spirit, she started her own investment firm. With a passion for simplifying personal finance, Harshada has helped countless clients set and achieve specific, measurable, attainable, relevant, and time-bound (SMART) financial goals. In her free time, Harshada enjoys reading and travelling to new destinations, which often inspires her innovative financial strategies.

Connect with Harshada Singh, Dignity Wealth For You/ Dignity Management Pvt Ltd:

Instagram: @harshada.singh.cfp
LinkedIn: www.linkedin.com/in/harshada-singh-cfp®-806a8063
Email : harshada@wealthforyou.in
Facebook: www.facebook.com/harshada.mahamane.7

***

Chaos to Clarity: Journey of Weaving Passions Together

Soniyaa Kapoor
Founder, Gyaanlekha Publishing / Light Language Healer & Spiritual Coach

---

You always showed interest in biology, wanted to become a doctor, graduated with a degree in mathematics, earned a diploma in digital marketing, and after at least five career changes, you are now a book publisher and a healer. Hasn't there been enough hopping and skipping for you to still be undecided? Are you a writer, a publisher, a spiritual coach, or a healer? Or can we finally call you an intelligent fool who has failed?

Welcome to the life of an adult who grew up as an introverted person navigating the challenges of complex family situations, depression, and immense pressure to succeed in conventional career paths. An adult who was good at everything yet could never decide what she truly wanted to do—until much later in life. Oh, and yes, this is the same adult who was once an intelligent child. Hi, I am Soniyaa Kapoor, a multi-passionate entrepreneur. It took me multiple career changes, plenty of failures, and a fair share of successes to finally be doing what I absolutely love.

You know how they say, "Don't work for money; do what you love." But what do you do when you love everything?

The Early Years

I was born into a family filled with trauma, and from childhood, I knew that wasn't going to be my story. I never felt truly connected to anyone growing up. I lived in my own world, daydreaming about my success as an adult. What I didn't realise then was how much it would shape who I would become in the future. But here's the thing: when you grow up with trauma and social injustice, you often become your own limitation without even realising it. I had dreams and hopes—not just random dreams but plans to escape the reality I was born into. I never felt like I belonged, and honestly, I never wanted to belong.

Right after graduation, I joined a medium-sized company as a Product Developer. It was my first real-world experience, and seeing people freely express themselves was a shock. At 20, I had no clear sense of self or awareness of my potential. With this, my journey of hard work began. I worked long hours, changed jobs frequently, and enjoyed the taste of success, earning promotions to Branch Manager and eventually Business Head. Those years helped me grow, honing skills I didn't know I had. I formed friendships and realised that life was more than limitations and trauma. I earned well, believed success would bring satisfaction, and thrived on the hustle.

The Next Phase- Introduction to doing something of your own!

Although I loved this new world of self-awareness and success, I soon realised I did not feel genuinely fulfilled. I reached a peak of burnout, and one day, after a sarcastic comment from my boss, I left my job in search of something that would truly fulfil my soul. The very next day, I attended a book launch event led by complete strangers. This is where I discovered the world of publishing. The publishing industry captivated me, especially self-publishing, where I noticed a glaring gap between authors and publishers. I wanted to bridge the gap between publishers and authors while giving opportunities to first-time authors who had something of value to share. I knew I could do it.

Attending that event and meeting authors and publishers invoked a curiosity within me. I did not have formal experience, but I had a deep desire to help people tell their stories. So, I spent a few months collaborating with other publishers, volunteering my time to learn the industry. While collaborating with authors, I got an opportunity to publish my own book. The book's quality turned out to be so low that I did not even bother collecting my complimentary copies. Despite collaborating with the publisher directly, I could not get an answer to this problem. They casually said, "We cannot give too much importance to authors. Quality does not matter. Authors should be grateful even to get a chance to be published." Once I had processed this shock and frustration, I decided to launch my own publishing company.

In the last nine years, I have published over thirty-five books on different topics and genres. Each one was a unique journey. From high school students to an 84-year-old debut writer, each project reminded me why I do what I do. Each story deserves to be told with care and excellence. Along with publishing books, I launched over 100 small to medium-sized writing challenges. I remember one of our virtual events that went on for over 12 hours.

Working with authors and launching new projects was deeply fulfilling, yet I wanted more. That feeling of something still missing was back. I soon realised I craved to integrate all the facets of myself—my spiritual gifts, my passion for healing, and my love for storytelling into a holistic business.

A significant turning point came during COVID. While the world slowed down, I found myself battling deep depression. I felt stuck, unsure of how to move forward. My business, though successful, did not fulfil me. The extra time at hand forced me into introspection. I began to see that this depression was not a setback. It was a call to heal myself and to start a new chapter.

The challenges we face in our entrepreneurial journey are not always setbacks or failures. These challenges come to the surface so we can go within and see where we are limiting ourselves, what negative stories we tell ourselves, and the environment by which we are surrounded. As entrepreneurs, our beliefs, living environment, past traumas, mental health, and values directly impact how we run our businesses and how much we succeed. So, while deeply challenging, I looked at my being overwhelmed and unfulfilled as an opportunity to explore within.

The Shift Toward Healing and Spirituality

While there were challenges and difficult days, I still enjoyed the world of books and publishing. One day, a friend gifted me a copy of a globally well-known book, The Secret. I smiled as I remembered reading that book when I had started working. Out of curiosity, I started reading it again. At that time, I was into personal development, which spoke of hardship and hard work. Reading this turned into a life-changing moment for me. As I read through the pages of this book, I felt the strange sensation of having known this information from somewhere before, but I could not place it. I had read this book before, but this information felt personal to me. Then I remembered how I used to daydream as a child. I recalled many past events, realising I was using visualisation without knowing it was called visualisation.

I started reading more and more books on spirituality and transformation. The more I read, the closer I felt to knowing my spiritual side. I realised that I was already using many principles of the Law of Attraction in my life.

Until this point, I was a rebel. I was raging. I wanted success as revenge for all the injustice I had witnessed as a child and in my growing years. This changed me as a person. It also changed me as an entrepreneur and how I showed up in my business and for my business. My success and my work became personal and sacred to me.

After another challenge involving my health, I found myself at rock bottom once more. By this time, I had become frustrated with constantly feeling unfulfilled and the never-ending challenges.

"*This can't be my story!*"

I screamed internally as I felt a mix of numbness and rage.

But as my mind kept shouting, "This can't be my story," something shifted inside me: *If this isn't my story, then what is?*

From that moment, my inner screams became my driving force. I declared to myself, "I need to heal. I need to be here for myself." It was not a sweetly worded affirmation but a fierce and raging intention. Sometimes, the path to transformation is not about calm mantras but raw, intense emotions. I realised that I did not need to suppress my anger or frustration—in fact, I could use it as fuel to shift my reality.

Through this period, I realised that some of the best manifestations happen when you are at your lowest point. It is not always about staying in a positive mindset; sometimes, the anger and frustration push you toward change. The truth is that even though I was helping others heal, manifest, and achieve their goals of writing and publishing, I was not growing much in my own life. This made me feel like a fraud for a while. I started doubting my own skills and capabilities.

My journey was not just about personal transformation; it marked the beginning of integrating spirituality into my entrepreneurial journey.

Merging My Passions into One Business

With this new realisation and shift in mindset, I began transforming myself both professionally and personally. I could see how special I was and the importance of what I added to people's lives through my work. I revisited how I had always worked hard and never had the confidence to ask for what I deserved, how I worked to shine bright yet hid when it was time to step into the light.

By 2020, I fully understood that my spiritual and healing gifts were not separate from my entrepreneurial path—they were integral to it. With each meditation, it became clearer to me that I did not need to choose between being a publisher and a spiritual coach. I could be both. In 2023, I rebranded my business, bringing together all of my skills. It was not an easy decision. In all these years, I had developed a connection with the name of my company and the brand I had created. It took a lot of courage. Here is the thing: the path of spiritual entrepreneurship isn't always logical; it demands absolute faith and inspired actions. Today, I run a publishing company that not only helps authors publish their books but also empowers them to explore their spiritual gifts. I coach and heal others while guiding them through their writing journeys.

Looking back, my story is not about a single career or title. It is about embracing all parts of myself: an entrepreneur, a healer, a coach, and letting them coexist. My journey taught me that success is not found in picking one passion but in weaving them together. My business now reflects that integration, and I could not be more aligned with my purpose.

There are many layers to one's entrepreneurial journey. I chose to share this part of my story because I encountered other entrepreneurs who, despite their potential, often felt a void and a lingering sense of unfulfillment. Being a multi-passionate person who chooses a creative path for entrepreneurship can often be challenging, and this journey can often feel lonely. Our childhood, family, friends, and living environment affect how we approach our business and how we deal with the problems we face on this journey.

We may not choose the traumas or challenges that shape us, but we do get to choose how we rise through them. For me, that rise came through entrepreneurship, spiritual healing, and helping others share their stories and journeys.

- Soniyaa Kapoor

~~~
~~~

AUTHOR INTRODUCTION

Soniyaa Kapoor is a Spiritual Coach, Light Language Healer, and Founder of Gyaanlekha Publishing. Born with spiritual, intuitive, and healing gifts, she guides people to manifest the life of their dreams through transformative coaching, healing practices, and various resources. Soniyaa combines her deep spiritual knowledge with her passion for storytelling, offering a unique blend of healing and creative expression.

At Gyaanlekha Publishing, she empowers entrepreneurs, coaches, and healers to embrace their spiritual gifts and share their stories with the world by publishing best-selling books that inspire and heal. With over nine years of experience in publishing, Soniyaa has helped bring more than 35 books to life, guiding authors in aligning their inner wisdom with their written work.

Her mission is to create a space where healing, spirituality, and writing come together, allowing individuals to heal from past traumas, discover their true potential, and manifest their highest visions.

When she's not coaching or publishing, you can find her immersed in meditation, enjoying a cup of tea, or creating beautiful art.

Connect with Soniyaa Kapoor, Gyaanlekha Publishing:

Instagram: @GyaanlekhaPublishing @soniyaakapoor
LinkedIn: www.linkedin.com/in/soniyaakapoor
www.linkedin.com/company/gyaanlekhapublishing
Facebook: www.facebook.com/GyaanlekhaPublishing
www.facebook.com/thesoniyaakapoor

***

Beyond the Stories

Introducing the Brands of Our Women Mavericks

GROW WITH SATORI

Grow with Satori is intended to enable awakening through self-discovery. Satori by definition, is a sudden enlightenment and a state of consciousness attained by intuitive illumination representing the spiritual goal of Zen Buddhism.

At Grow with Satori, we are driven by our core values—Growth, Respect, Integrity, Collaboration, and Excellence (GRICE). These values are the foundation of our programs and learning journeys, ensuring that you achieve your desired goals.

Our mission is clear: to make workplaces better for people, teams, and organisations by enabling self-discovery, empowering individuals, and elevating communities. With your unwavering support, we are excited to present the latest insights, tools, and inspiration to help you thrive in both your personal and professional life.

Grow with Satori specialises in creating Learning Journeys that are carefully and intentionally crafted to cater to a blend of modalities and learning preferences. Each offering weaves a blend of interventions into a well-thought-through journey and may include: Instructor-led sessions (both Virtual and In-person training), coaching (one on one, group, and team coaching), self-study (articles or videos), project work (individual projects or action learning projects in teams), quizzes, games, research, journaling, activities (involving psychodrama and art), and community or social activities that lead to phenomenal learning.

We also support learning through various assessments such as the Harrison Assessment, Belbin Team Roles, Gallup Strengths Finder, DiSC, and Interaction Styles Assessment. Each of these reports offers holistic awareness about oneself and can complement several learning interventions. We are equipped to use these in skill-building as appropriate.

The various modalities and interventions available make it possible for learners with any learning style to cope with and stay abreast of the curriculum. Such learning journeys are empowering to the learner and boost confidence.

Grow with Satori and its partners hope to impart knowledge and learning and walk with you through coaching to enable you to attain your Zen goal... Satori!

Connect With Grow with Satori:

Webpage: www.growithsatori.com
Email: shanti@growithsatori.com
Linktree: www.linktr.ee/growtihsatori
Instagram: www.instagram.com/growithsatori
Twitter: www.twitter.com/LearningSatori
Facebook: www.facebook.com/growithsatori

READERS ADDA

In today's digital age, nurturing a love for reading in children is more essential than ever. Jyoti Dora, the founder of Readers Adda, recognised this need and embarked on a mission to connect children with books, offering an alternative to excessive screen time. With a background as a certified storyteller, NLP practitioner, Transformation Coach, and holder of a Master's Degree in Human Resource Development (MHRD), Jyoti combines her extensive experience in education and corporate sectors to promote a holistic approach to learning.

Readers Adda reflects Jyoti's passion for education and societal impact. The initiative fosters a love for reading while guiding parents on creating a supportive reading environment. Even during the COVID-19 pandemic, Jyoti extended her reach through online sessions, impacting children in marginalised areas and earning recognition from the World Talent Organization, USA. With over 20 years of experience, Jyoti continues to shape the future by cultivating reading habits that enhance cognitive abilities and character development in children.

Connect with Readers Adda:

Webpage: www.readersadda.co.in
Email: jyotidora21@gmail.com
LinkedIn: www.linkedin.com/in/jyoti-dora-67230719b
Facebook: www.facebook.com/readersaddasurat
Instagram: jyotidora.readersadda

UNIQAYA LIFESTYLE

At Uniqaya, we believe that skincare should be as pure and purposeful as nature itself. Our journey began with a simple yet profound mission: to create clean, functional skincare that truly makes a difference.

With over 40 years of experience in the pharmaceutical industry, Uniqaya bridges the power of nature and the precision of science to craft products that are effective, safe, and aligned with our commitment to clean beauty. Our dedication to harnessing nature's best ensures that your skin gets the care it deserves, bringing out the beauty within.

Thanks to the overwhelming support of our customers, Uniqaya has been proudly featured in prestigious publications like Hindustan Times, Femina, CXO, Deccan Herald, Glittering India, Women Entrepreneur, Pinkvilla, and more. Furthermore, our founder, Dr Gagaan, has been honoured as one of the Top 30 Women Entrepreneurs of 2023 by Indian Alert.

Connect with Uniqaya Lifestyle:

Instagram: @uniqayalifestyle
Facebook: www.facebook.com/Uniqayalifestyle
LinkedIn: www.linkedin.com/company/uniqayalifestyle
Website: www.uniqaya.com

PIHARWA

Piharwa is a retail fashion brand that celebrates India's rich tradition and craftsmanship. Specializing in handloom sarees and handcrafted lifestyle products, each piece reflects the artistry and heritage of Indian artisans. Piharwa curates diverse styles and weaving techniques, honouring cultural traditions while uplifting skilled craftsmen.

With a mission to blend tradition with modern style, Piharwa offers a range of elegant sarees, lehengas, poshaks, and trendy Indo-Western collections. The brand is deeply committed to sustainability, valuing the beauty of natural fibres and the intricate artistry of handlooms.

Piharwa also extends its vision into home décor through its sister brand, Elements of Piharwa, which draws inspiration from Indian craft traditions. Together, these brands empower customers to embrace fashion and home décor, reflecting India's cultural legacy.

Piharwa is more than a brand—it's a tribute to India's artisans, weaving tradition and craftsmanship into every creation.

Connect with Piharwa:

Linktree: https://linktr.ee/jprakriti
Instagram: @piharwa
YouTube: www.youtube.com/@piharwabhopal7402

MAHASVANA

Mahasvana, derived from the Sanskrit word meaning "great sound", addresses the challenges encountered by individuals who, despite having access to abundant opportunities, frequently struggle with a lack of motivation to take full advantage of them. Far more than a source of fleeting inspiration, Mahasvana offers powerful and relatable content that speaks directly to the needs of today's generation. By providing actionable advice that resonates deeply, it empowers individuals to unlock their true potential and achieve lasting transformation.

Through compelling real-world stories, hands-on exercises, and proven strategies, Mahasvana equips individuals with essential tools needed to cultivate long-term habits for success. Rooted in the belief that motivation, like sound, should reverberate powerfully, Mahasvana strives to create a ripple effect of positive change.

More than just a course provider, Mahasvana is dedicated to being a lifelong partner in personal development. It ensures learners embark on a transformative journey, where motivation evolves into a sustainable, life-enhancing habit—helping people confidently pursue their goals and live with purpose.

Connect with Mahasvana:

Webpage: www.mahasvana.com
YouTube: www.youtube.com/@mahasvanamotivation
Email: info@mahasvana.com
LinkedIn: https://www.linkedin.com/in/soundarya-lahari

PRACHITEE EXPERIENTIAL SCHOOL

Prachitee Experiential School located in Whitefield, Bangalore is an award winning, innovative preschool with a vision to create lifelong learners.

At Prachitee, we believe that education is not just about imparting knowledge but about nurturing each student's unique potential and helping them grow into well-rounded individuals.

Our logo, which depicts a blossoming child, represents this belief. The "प्र" of Prachitee is modelled into a tree to signify a strong foundation that we provide in Prachitee. It represents the transformation that takes place when children are given the right environment and resources to thrive.

Our mission is to seed young children with love for learning, foster critical thinking and equip them with 21st Century skills and our inhouse Project Based Experiential Learning (PBEL) curriculum is built around this. The PBEL curriculum focuses on hands-on learning through projects and activities which promote creativity, critical thinking and problem-solving skills.

Prachitee is not just a school, it's a community. We strive to create a community that not only values academic achievement but also promotes social and emotional growth.
Come be part of this community!

Connect with Prachitee Experiential School:

Webpage: www.prachitee.com
Email: prachiteeschool@gmail.com
Instagram: @prachitee_education
Facebook: www.facebook.com/ProjectBasedExperientialLearning

FOOD MONK CONSULTANTS LLP

Food Monk Consultants is a premier consultancy firm that specialises in supporting both start-ups and established food processing businesses with research and development, product innovation, and successful market launches. The firm guides clients from concept through to commissioning, ensuring a seamless transition from idea to market-ready product.

With expertise across various sectors of the food processing industry—including dairy and dairy products, chocolate and confectionery, millet-based products, ready-to-eat/ready-to-cook foods, and beverages—Food Monk Consultants is well-equipped to address diverse needs. Based in Pune, Maharashtra, the firm operates across India and internationally, providing comprehensive support wherever clients are located.

Connect with Food Monk Consultants LLP:

Website: www.foodmonkconsultant.com
Instagram: @foodmonkconsultants
LinkedIn: www.linkedin.com/company/food-monk-consultants
Facebook: www.facebook.com/people/Food-Monk-Consultants/100071089193432

DIGNITY WEALTH FOR YOU/ DIGNITY MANAGEMENT PVT LTD

Dignity Wealth For You/ Dignity Management Pvt Ltd offers comprehensive wealth management solutions to individuals, families, businesses, and other entities. We have had our expertise in this field for over a decade now. We provide tailored strategies to help clients achieve their financial goals, simplifying the complexities of investment decisions. Committed to long-term wealth creation, Dignity Wealth For You empowers individuals and families to build a secure and prosperous financial future.

Connect with Dignity Wealth For You/ Dignity Management Pvt Ltd:

Instagram: @harshada.singh.cfp
LinkedIn: www.linkedin.com/in/harshada-singh-cfp®-806a8063
Email: harshada@wealthforyou.in
Website: www.wealthforyou.in

GYAANLEKHA PUBLISHING

Gyaanlekha Publishing specialises in non-fiction book publishing for coaches, healers, and spiritual entrepreneurs. We empower individuals in fields like spirituality, holistic living, and self-help to share their expertise and transform lives through impactful books. With personalised guidance and a deep understanding of our client's unique journeys, we help craft meaningful works that establish them as thought leaders.

At GyaanLekha, we also provide resources and tools on spirituality, healing, meditation, and self-development through eBooks, free downloads, courses, and workshops. Our mission is to bring forth books that inspire, heal, and guide readers in manifesting their highest potential.

Connect with Gyaanlekha Publishing:

Instagram: @GyaanlekhaPublishing @soniyaakapoor
LinkedIn: www.linkedin.com/in/soniyaakapoor
www.linkedin.com/company/gyaanlekhapublishing
Facebook: www.facebook.com/GyaanlekhaPublishing
www.facebook.com/thesoniyaakapoor

***

ACKNOWLEDGEMENT

We would like to express our deepest gratitude to all the extraordinary entrepreneurs who opened their hearts, shared their journeys, and inspired us with their honesty and courage. Your willingness to reveal not only your triumphant moments but also your vulnerable ones when things didn't go as planned or when you faced failure has created something truly powerful. Your strength and authenticity have shaped this beautiful book.

Lastly, to our readers: may this book serve as a beacon of hope and inspiration. Through the pages of these stories, we hope you'll discover not only the resilience within these women but also the immense power within yourself.

With heartfelt appreciation,
Gyaanlekha Publishing

THANK YOU!

***

***

***